WONDERFUL WIRE JEWELRY

MAKE 30+ BRACELETS, EARRINGS, NECKLACES, AND MORE

Erica Swanson

Kalmbach Books

WAUKESHA, WI

Kalmbach Books
21027 Crossroads Circle
Waukesha, Wisconsin 53186
www.JewelryAndBeadingStore.com

Published in 2016
20 19 18 17 16   1 2 3 4 5

Manufactured in China

ISBN: 978-1-62700-004-8
EISBN: 978-1-62700-189-2

The material in this book has appeared previously in *Wirework* magazine. *Wirework* is registered as a trademark.

Editor: Erica Swanson
Book Design: Carole Ross
Illustrator: Kellie Jaeger
Photographers: James Forbes and William Zuback

Library of Congress Control Number: 2015941325

CONTENTS

Introduction 4

Basics

Contributors 111

Projects

BRACELETS & CUFFS

NECKLACES & PENDANTS

EARRINGS & RINGS

INTRODUCTION

Wirework is a wonderfully versatile craft. It can be as simple as adding a loop to a beaded headpin for a lovely pair of earrings—or as complex as an intricately woven and wrapped bracelet. You can work with the material itself to create beautiful pieces, or add beads and wrap cabochons for color. The possibilities are endless!

Depending on your budget and taste, you may love the warmth and interesting patina that copper gives to a piece—or you may prefer to work with shiny, bright silver. Perhaps you're looking for a quick pair of earrings. Maybe you're ready to make a cuff dripping with wired style.

The talented designers included in *Wonderful Wire Jewelry* offer a wide range of styles and techniques for you to try. Clear, easy-to-follow, step-by-step photos will guide you through each project for the best results. You can flip to the Basics section at the back of the book if you are unfamiliar with a term or technique.

Whatever projects you choose, have fun making and wearing them.

Erica Swanson
Associate Editor, Kalmbach Books

BRACELETS
&
CUFFS

Entwined hearts bracelet

Hammering these simple links creates a charming string of hearts, and the clever clasp is just an unopened link! Experiment with wire gauges to vary the look.

by Janice Berkebile

materials

Bracelet 7 in. (17.8 cm)

- 40 in. (1.2 m) 14-gauge (1.6 mm) copper wire, round, dead soft

tools & supplies

- Wirework toolbox, p. 105
- Flush cutters strong enough to cut 14-gauge (1.6 mm) wire
- Stepped roundnose pliers
- Liver of sulfur
- Pro-Polish polishing pad
- Sunshine polishing cloth

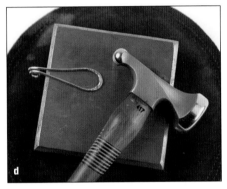

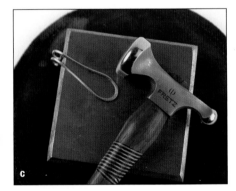

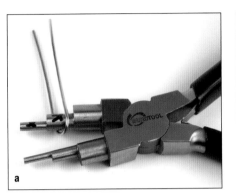

Scroll links

1 For each link in the bracelet, flush-cut a 5-in. (12.7 cm) piece of 14-gauge wire. For a 7-in. (17.8 cm) bracelet, you'll need eight links. Center each wire on the middle tier of the large jaw of the stepped roundnose pliers. Bend the wire around the jaw so that the ends meet evenly **(a)**.

2 Using the smallest tier of the large jaw, grasp both ends of the wire, and roll the pliers away from you until the ends touch the base wire to form a loop **(b)**.

3 Place the link on a steel bench block with the loops hanging off the edge and facing down. With the flat face of a chasing hammer, flatten the curve opposite the loops **(c)**, and texture the curve with the round face **(d)**.

4 With the middle tier of the large jaw of the pliers, grasp the two ends close to the loops. Roll the loops toward the curved end **(e)** in the opposite direction of the loops. The finished scroll links will look like this **(f)**.

Assembly

5 Choose the link that has the most space in the curved end to be the loop half of the clasp. Slide the curved end of another link over the two loops of the clasp link **(g)**.

6 Continue attaching the links until the bracelet is the desired length **(h)**.

7 Skipping the last link you added (this will be the hook end of the clasp), use flatnose pliers to bend both scroll-link arches to the side to flatten the link, creating the heart shape **(i)**. Do this for the remaining links. Tweak each link with chainnose and roundnose pliers until they're uniform and the small loops are closed and touching **(j)**. Bend up the curved end of each link slightly to ensure that the bracelet lies flat and is flexible.

8 Place the arches of the links on the bench block. Flatten and texture the arches with the chasing hammer **(k)**.

9 Patinate the bracelet with liver of sulfur (Basics, p. 110). Clean the bracelet with a polishing pad, and polish it with a polishing cloth.

TIP

If you don't have stepped roundnose pliers, you can substitute standard roundnose and long roundnose pliers. Use the tip of the standard roundnose for the first set of loops and the base of the long roundnose to make the second set of loops. The advantage of the stepped roundnose pliers is that you can make both loops at the same time. Whichever pliers you use, mark them with a fine-tip permanent marker to remind yourself where to grasp the wire so your loops are consistent.

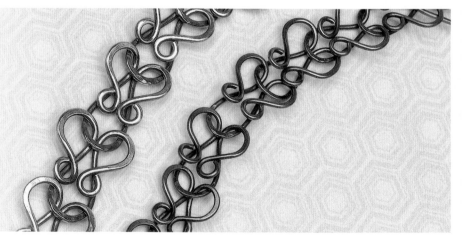

The links in the 14-gauge bracelet (left) are ¾ in. (19 mm) wide. The 16-gauge bracelet (right) has ½-in. (13 mm) links.

Bombay bracelet

Highlight a large crystal stone in a framework of twisted and straight square wire.

by Debra Saucier

materials

Bracelet 2½-in. (64 mm) diameter
- Sterling silver wire: 20-gauge (0.81 mm), square, half-hard, 7 ft. (2.1 m)
- 20 x 30 mm foiled-back crystal stone (Swarovski #4127)

tools & supplies
- Wirework toolbox, p. 105
- Nylon-jaw pliers (optional)
- 2 pin vises
- Painter's tape
- Bracelet mandrel (optional)

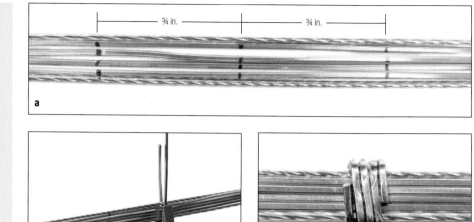

a

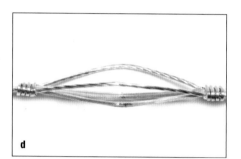

b

c

1 Cut six 10-in. (25.4 cm) pieces of 20-gauge (0.81 mm) square wire. Straighten the wires with nylon-jaw pliers or a polishing cloth. Using two pin vises, twist two of the wires (Basics, p. 109).

Align the six wires next to each other with a twisted wire at each outer edge. Secure each end of the band of wires with painter's tape. Mark the center of the band with a permanent marker. Make a mark ¾ in. (19 mm) to each side of the center mark **(a)**.

2 Using chainnose pliers, make a hook about 1 in. (25.5 mm) from the end of a 4-in. (10.2 cm) piece of square wire. Place the hook on one of the outer marks on the band, and use flatnose pliers to squeeze the hook in place **(b)**.

d

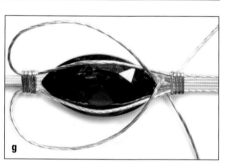

e

3 Working toward the nearest end of the band, fold the long end of the wire over the band, and use flatnose pliers to squeeze the wire in place. Making sure the band wires stay flat, continue folding and squeezing the wire around the band until you've made four wraps.

Using flush cutters, trim each end of the wrapping wire on the same surface of the band, and squeeze the ends against the band. The side where the wrapping wires are trimmed will be the back of the bracelet.

Repeat steps 2 and 3 at the band's remaining outer mark **(c)**.

4 Lift the twisted wires on the band slightly to allow a focal stone to fit under them **(d)**. Using roundnose pliers, gently separate the remaining four band wires into two pairs, creating a diamond-shaped opening about ¾ in. (19 mm) wide **(e)**. Position the stone under the twisted wires with its back sitting in the diamond-shaped opening **(f)**. Using chainnose pliers, gently pinch the wires together just above and below the stone.

f

g

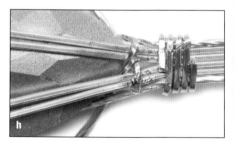

h

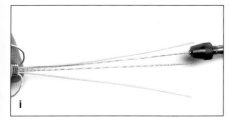

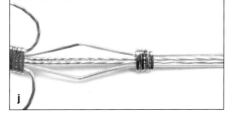

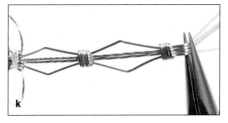

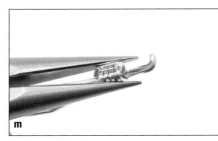

5 Release one end of the wires from the painter's tape. Gently curve each outer twisted wire around the stone, forming a narrow heart shape. Insert each wire end into the space between the stone and the adjacent set of wraps **(g)**.

6 Wrap each wire tail around the adjacent pair of band wires, and trim **(h)**.

Repeat steps 5 and 6 on the other side of the band.

7 On each side, use a pin vise to twist the middle two band wires **(i)**.

8 Mark each side of the band 1 in. (25.5 mm) from the previous sets of wraps. Make a hook at the end of a 4-in. (10.2 cm) piece of square wire, and, working as in step 3, make four wraps at one of the marks. Repeat on the other side.

On each side, mark the center between the sets of wraps. On one side, use chainnose pliers to pull each outer wire at the mark, creating a diamond-shaped opening about ¾ in. (19 mm) wide. Repeat on the other side **(j)**.

Repeat to make a second diamond-shaped segment on each side.

9 On one side, grasp the band wires about 7 mm (¼ in.) from the last set of wraps, and bend the wires 90 degrees toward the back of the band **(k)**. Cut the wires about ¹⁄₁₆ in. (1.5 mm) from the bend **(l)**. Bend the tail of each wire over the last set of wraps **(m)** and squeeze the wires. Repeat at the other end of the band.

Use a bracelet mandrel or your fingers to shape the band into an oval.

Woven wire ripple cuff

Connect shaped and woven wire frames to make a lightweight cuff with great curves. Embellish the design with a few beads at the intersections of the frames and fanciful spirals at the ends.

by Lisa Claxton

materials

Cuff 2½-in. (64 mm) diameter

- Sterling silver wire: 20-gauge (0.81 mm), round, half-hard, 5 ft. (1.5 m)
- Fine-silver wire: 26-gauge (0.4 mm), round, dead-soft, 33 ft. (10.1 m) (½ oz.)
- 6 6–8 mm flat-back or coin-shaped beads

tools & supplies

- Wirework toolbox, p. 105
- Finger-Pro tape
- Ring clamp (optional)
- Wire jig
- Liver of sulfur (optional)

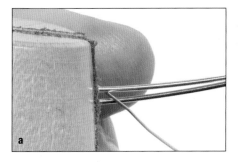

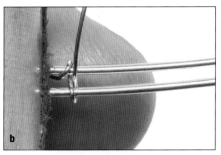

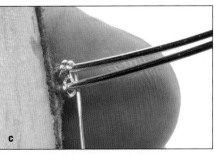

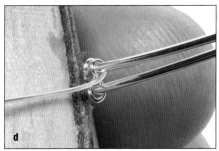

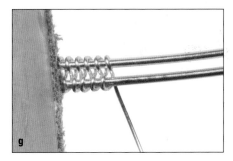

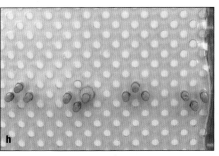

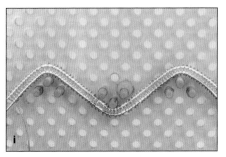

The weaving process is very hard on the fingers. To prevent injury, wrap the forefinger and thumb of your dominant hand with tape before you start weaving.

Frame segments

1 Cut two 15-in. (38.1 cm) pieces of 20-gauge (0.81 mm) wire; these will be the core wires. If desired, run them through nylon-jaw pliers to straighten them. Cut 12 ft. (3.7 m) of 26-gauge (0.4 mm) weaving wire.

Hold the core wires together so the ends are even. Position the weaving wire between the core wires about 4 in. (10.2 cm) from one end of the core wires. Place the core wires in a ring clamp adjacent to the weaving wire, if desired. The ring clamp isn't necessary, but it helps to reduce hand fatigue **(a)**.

2 Tightly bring the weaving wire over the top wire, between the core wires, under the bottom wire, and back between the core wires **(b)**.

3 From this point on, weave the wire

in four rhythmic motions for each row:
- Tightly bring the weaving wire over the top core wire **(c)**.
- Pull the weaving wire firmly between the core wires, locking it in place with a thumbnail or fingernail **(d)**.
- Tightly bring the weaving wire under the bottom core wire **(e)**.
- Pull the weaving wire firmly between the core wires, locking it in place with a thumbnail or fingernail **(f)**.

4 Continue weaving as in step 3 until the woven segment is about 8 in. (20.3 cm). To keep your work straight and even, reposition your gripping hand or the ring clamp close to the weaving every ½ in.

(13 mm) or so **(g)**.

Repeat steps 1–4 to make another frame segment.

Shaping the frame segments

5 Position pegs in a wire jig as shown **(h)**.

6 Keeping a frame segment flat against the jig, guide it around the peg groups to make a total of seven bends. Most jigs are smaller than the length of the frame segments, so you'll probably have to reposition the frame segments to complete the shaping. Use nylon-jaw pliers to flatten the frame segments against the jig as needed **(i)**.

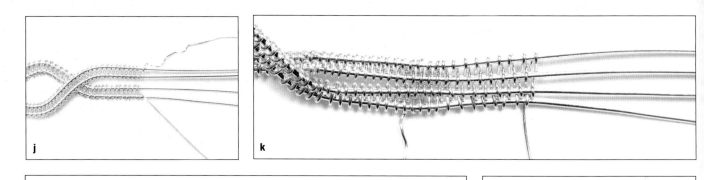

j

k

l

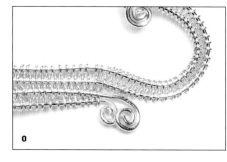

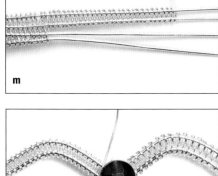

m

n

o

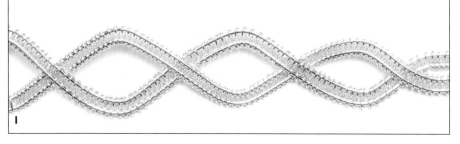

p

7 Place one frame segment on top of the other with the bends going in opposite directions. At one end, bend the frames right after the last intersection so the four core wires are parallel. If necessary, add or remove weaving wire on one or both frame segments so the weaving ends at the same place **(j)**.

8 Cut 3 ft. (91.4 cm) of weaving wire, and wrap it once around the top core wire. Weave it over the next core wire, under the following core wire, and around the bottom core wire. Continue weaving under and over the core wires for about ½ in. (13 mm) to join them **(k)**.

9 Alternately cross the frame segments at the intersection points. Gently shape the bracelet around your wrist, and repeat step 8 to join the other end. Test the fit. The clasp will add about 1 in. (25.5 mm), so add or remove rows of weaving at each joined section as needed to create the desired length **(l)**.

Clasp and finishing

10 On one end, continue weaving one pair of core wires for about 1 in. (25.5 mm). Repeat at the other end of the bracelet, but extend the weaving on the other pair of wires **(m)**.

11 On one end, shape the 1-in. (25.5 mm) woven section into a hook. Cut each of the hook's core wires ¾ in. (19 mm) from the end of the woven section. Using roundnose and chainnose pliers, make a spiral (Basics, p. 109) on the end of each core wire **(n)**.

12 On this end of the bracelet, there are two remaining core wires. Cut the bottom core wire about ½ in. (13 mm) from the woven section and the inner core wire about ¾ in. (19 mm) from the woven section. Work as in step 11 to shape each wire end into a spiral facing away from the frame.
  Repeat steps 11 and 12 at the other end the bracelet, positioning the hook in the opposite direction from the first one.

Trim any remaining wire tails flush against the back side of the cuff, and use chainnose pliers to flatten them **(o)**.

13 Center a 6–8 mm bead on 6 in. (15.2 cm) of wrapping wire. Position the bead at one intersection on the frame. Using one end of the wrapping wire, make at least two wraps around both frame segments. If possible, try to nestle the wrapping wire into the spaces in the weaving on the frame to give the wire a good grip. Repeat with the other wire end, going in the other direction **(p)**. Trim the wire tails flush, and flatten them.
  Repeat at the remaining five intersections, then gently finish shaping your cuff.
  If desired, patinate your bracelet using liver of sulfur according to the manufacturer's instructions.

Uncommon wraps

Coil and weave a colorful assortment of components, and arrange them on a sturdy base. Lash the units in place with a loopy edging.

by Lisa Niven Kelly

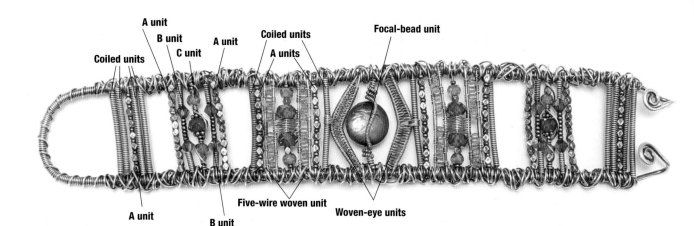

A unit
B unit
C unit
A unit
Coiled units
A units
Coiled units
Focal-bead unit
A unit
B unit
Five-wire woven unit
Woven-eye units

materials

Bracelet 2½–3-in. (64–76 mm) diameter

- Sterling silver wire:
  - 14-gauge (1.63 mm), dead-soft, 2 ft. (61 cm)
  - 20-gauge (0.81 mm) scrap wire, half-hard, 14 in. (35.6 cm)
  - 22-gauge (0.64 mm), half-hard, 25 ft. (7.6 m)
  - 24-gauge (0.51 mm), half-hard, 13 ft. (4 m)
  - 28-gauge (0.32 mm), dead-soft, 12 ft. (3.7 m)
- 12–15 mm focal bead
- **200–250** 2–5 mm accent beads
- 1 g 15º or 11º seed beads
- **4** 4 mm daisy or star spacers

tools & supplies

- Wirework toolbox, p. 105
- Ring clamp

Flex your creativity and customize your bracelet to suit your tastes, or follow my design as shown above.

Preparation

Coils

To make coils (Basics, p. 109), center 12 ft. (3.7 m) of 24-gauge (0.51 mm) wrapping wire on a piece of 20-gauge (0.81 mm) scrap wire. Make wraps around the scrap wire, keeping them tight, until you have 6 in. (15.2 cm) of coil. Trim the wrapping-wire tail. Working on the other side of the scrap wire, repeat to wrap the rest of the scrap wire. Remove the coil from the scrap wire.

Cut twelve ⁷⁄₈-in. (22 mm) pieces from the coil. Set the remaining coil aside to use later.

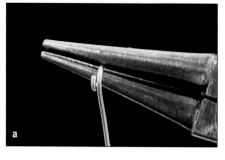

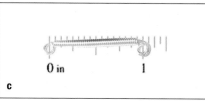

Coiled units

1 Cut 2 in. (51 mm) of 22-gauge (0.64 mm) wire; this will be your core wire. Using roundnose pliers, grasp one end of the core wire, positioning the pliers so they will make a loop big enough to later fit on 14-gauge (1.63 mm) wire. Make a loop and a half, turning so the tip of the wire goes toward the tip of the pliers **(a)**.

2 Slide a ⁷⁄₈-in. (22 mm) coil onto the core wire, and make a loop and a half in the same direction as the first loop **(b)**. The coiled unit should measure exactly 1 in. (25.5 mm) between the centers of the loops **(c)**.

Repeat steps 1 and 2 with the remaining 11 coils, making sure they're all the same length.

A, B, and C units

3 Follow steps 1 and 2, but instead of stringing a coil, string beads as desired. I made beaded units as follows:

- A units: String ⁷⁄₈ in. (22 mm) of 2 mm beads **(d)**. Make a total of 10 A units (six

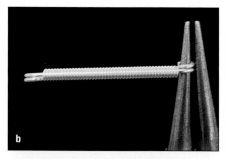

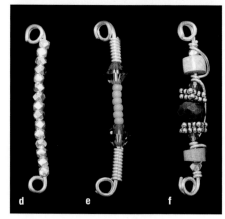

in one pattern and four in another).

- B units: String a ⅛-in. (3 mm) coil, a 4 mm bead, ¼ in. (6 mm) of 15º or 11º seed beads, a 4 mm bead, and a ⅛-in. (3 mm) coil **(e)**. Make a total of four B units.

- C units: String ¾ in. (19 mm) of assorted beads. This leaves a little space on the core wire to add decorative wrapping: Cut 3 in. (76 mm) of 24-gauge (0.51 mm) wrapping wire. Make a couple of wraps at one end of the core wire. Skipping over the next one or more beads, make a wrap around the core wire. Repeat twice, and trim the wrapping wire **(f)**. Make a total of two C units.

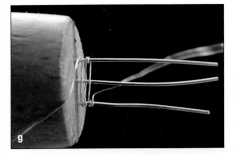

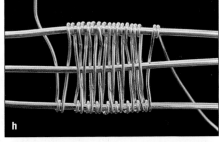

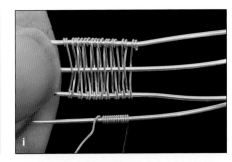

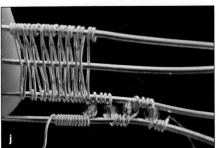

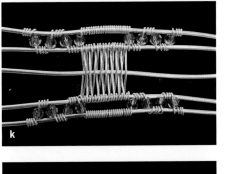

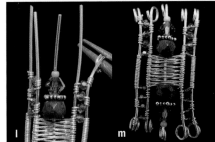

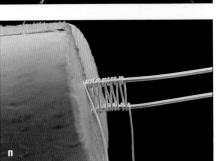

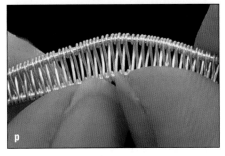

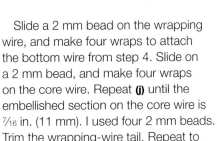

Five-wire woven units

4 Cut three 2-in. (51 mm) pieces of 22-gauge (0.64 mm) core wire. Insert the end 1 in. (25.5 mm) of the three wires into a ring clamp, spacing them ⅛ in. (3 mm) apart.

Center 15 in. (38.1 cm) of 28-gauge (0.32 mm) wrapping wire over the top wire next to the clamp. Bring the wire down, in front of the center wire, and behind the bottom wire. Make one wrap around the bottom wire, then go behind the center wire and in front of the top wire. Make one wrap around the top wire. Continue weaving **(h)** until the woven section is ⅛ in. (3 mm). Flip the wires in the clamp, and weave the other end **(i)**. Trim the wrapping-wire tails.

5 Cut 2 in. (51 mm) of 22-gauge (0.64 mm) core wire and 12 in. (30.5 cm) of 28-gauge (0.32 mm) wrapping wire. Align the core wire with the three wires from step 4. Center the wrapping wire at the middle of the core wire, and make a ⅛-in. (3 mm) coil **(j)**.

Slide a 2 mm bead on the wrapping wire, and make four wraps to attach the bottom wire from step 4. Slide on a 2 mm bead, and make four wraps on the core wire. Repeat **(j)** until the embellished section on the core wire is ⁷⁄₁₆ in. (11 mm). I used four 2 mm beads. Trim the wrapping-wire tail. Repeat to embellish the other side of the core wire.

Repeat to add a fifth core wire **(k)**.

6 String beads on the center wire so the top bead is flush with the outer embellishments. Make a loop at the end of each wire **(l)** as before. Repeat at the other end of the unit **(m)**. Make a total of two woven units.

Note: When I finished this unit, the center wire was longer than the rest, so I used chainnose pliers to break the end seed beads and then adjusted my loops so the wire was the right length.

Woven-eye component

7 Cut two 2½-in. (64 mm) pieces of 22-gauge (0.64 mm) core wire.

Insert the end 1¼ in. (32 mm) of each wire in the clamp, spacing them ⅛ in. (3 mm) apart.

Center 24 in. (61 cm) of 28-gauge (0.32 mm) wrapping wire over the top wire next to the clamp. Bring the wrapping wire in front of the bottom wire, and make one wrap. Bring it in front of the top wire, and make one wrap. Continue **(n)** until the woven section is ½ in. (13 mm). If desired, taper the component by letting the ends of the core wires get closer together. Flip the core wires in the clamp, and repeat to weave the other side **(o)**. Trim the wrapping-wire tails.

8 Bend the woven segment slightly at the center to form a boomerang shape **(p)**. Using your fingernails, make a gap in the weaving at the outer edge of the bend **(q)**. Make loops at the ends of the core wires as before.

Make another woven-eye component in the mirror image of the first.

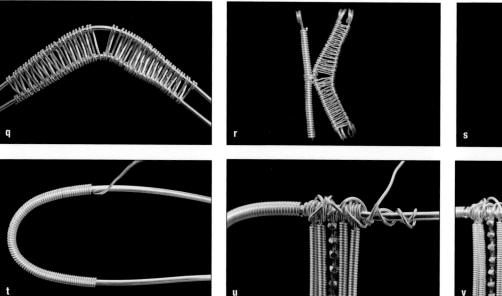

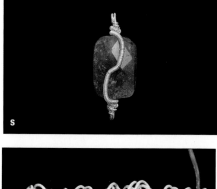

9 Using 2 in. (51 mm) of 28-gauge (0.32 mm) wrapping wire, make several wraps to lash the outer bend of a woven-eye unit to a coiled unit. Repeat with the other woven-eye unit **(r)**.

Focal-bead unit

10 Cut 5 in. (12.7 cm) of 24-gauge (0.51 mm) wire and 18 in. (45.7 cm) of 28-gauge (0.32 mm) wrapping wire. Center the wrapping wire on the 24-gauge (0.51 mm) wire, and wrap it to make a coil.

Cut 2 in. (51 mm) of 22-gauge (0.64 mm) core wire, and make a loop on one end as in step 2. Wrap the coil around the core wire twice. String a focal bead. Skipping over the focal bead, wrap the coil around the other end of the core wire. Trim the coil.

Making sure the unit is the same length as the others, make a loop to finish it. If desired, make decorative bends in the coil **(s)**.

Assembly

11 Measure your wrist ½ in. (13 mm) above your wrist bone, and add 1 in. (25.5 mm) to determine the total length of your bracelet (from the outer edge of the hooks to the outer edge of the loop).

Bend 2 ft. (61 cm) of 14-gauge (1.63 mm) wire so the ends are parallel and 1 in. (25.5 mm) apart; this will be your base wire. Measuring from the

bend, mark the bracelet length on the wire ends, then mark the center point between the bend and the marks you just made. Don't trim the wire ends; you'll use these to complete the hooks.

Cut 3 ft. (91.4 cm) of 22-gauge (0.64 mm) wrapping wire, and wrap it around the base wire to make a 2½-in. (64 mm) coil. Slide the coil so it covers the bend. Don't trim the wrapping wire **(t)**.

12 Slide the coiled and beaded units onto the base wire as desired, making sure the loops all face the same direction. Snug the units close to the coil made in step 11, and loop the wrapping wire around the base and in

between the units to make loopy sculptural wraps. Continue wrapping past the units to create a gap before the next group of units. Wrap back over the first layer of wraps to make the edging as loopy as desired **(u)**.

13 Slide the next set of units up to the wrapping wire, and continue wrapping as in step 12.

When the wrapping wire gets short, slide it under a nearby loop, and trim. To continue wrapping, cut 2–3 ft. (61–91.4 cm) of wrapping wire, and anchor it to the base where you ended your previous wire. Continue wrapping loosely around the base and between the units, sliding the next set of

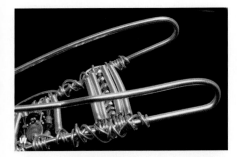 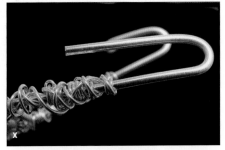

Process photos by Lisa Niven Kelly.

components up as needed. Make sure the focal bead sits at the center mark.

Finish the second side as a mirror image of the first. Position the last set of units about ¾ in. (19 mm) from the bracelet length mark.

Anchor a new piece of wrapping wire on the other edge of the base, and wrap it as you did the first edge **(v)**.

Double hook clasp

14 Using roundnose pliers, grasp an end mark on one wire, and pull the wire over the pliers toward the front surface of the band to make a hook. Repeat with the other wire **(w)**.

15 Trim each wire so that ¼ in. (6 mm) overlaps the sculptural loops **(x)**.

16 Grasp the very tip of one wire with the tip of your chainnose pliers, and bend the wire into a tight, slightly open loop **(y)**. Pinch the loop closed with chainnose pliers **(z)**. Repeat on the other wire.

17 Gently bend the band into a bracelet shape with your hands. To clasp the bracelet, pinch the hooks together slightly, and slide them through the loop. As an option, you may wrap the hooks together with 22-gauge (0.64 mm) wire **(aa)**.

note

For an antiqued look, you can either patinate your wire before you begin working or patinate the bracelet after you've made it. Patinated wire will polish up as you work. If you patinate the bracelet, polish it in a tumbler.

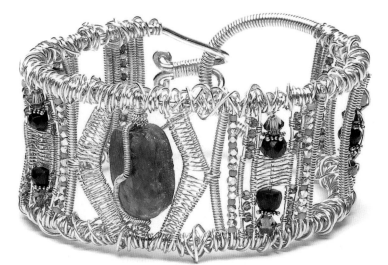

Curves & waves bracelet

Capture pearls in the graceful curves of flat aluminum wire.

by Monica Han

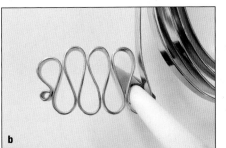

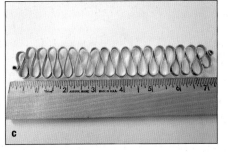

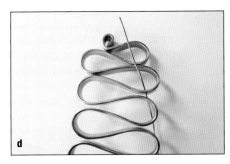

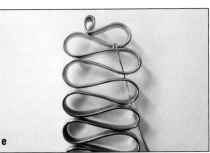

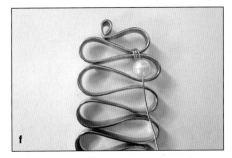

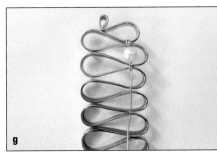

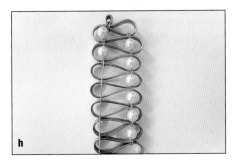

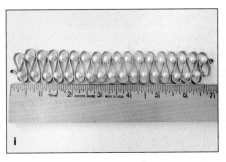

Bracelet base

1 Flush-cut 5 ft. (1.5 m) of 16-gauge flat wire. Using roundnose pliers, make a small loop at one end. About ½ in. (13 mm) from the loop, wrap the wire around an 8 mm pen or other round mandrel to make a curve **(a)**.

materials

Bracelet 7 in. (17.8 cm)

- 5½ ft. (1.7 m) 16-gauge (1.3 mm) 4 mm wide flat aluminum wire
- 4½ ft. (1.4 m) 24-gauge (0.5 mm) round copper wire
- **33** 6 mm crystal pearls (Swarovski, white)

tools & supplies

- Nylon-jaw pliers (optional)
- Roundnose pliers
- Flush cutters strong enough to cut 16-gauge (1.3 mm) wire
- 8 mm diameter pen or other round mandrel

2 About 1 in. (25.5 mm) from the previous curve, make another curve. Continue making curves every 1 in. (25.5 mm) as shown **(b)** for the desired length bracelet minus ½ in. (13 mm) for the clasp. Make one last curve ½ in. (13 mm) from the previous curve. Using roundnose pliers, make a small loop at this end **(c)**.

Wrapping

3 Cut a 24-in. (61 cm) piece of 24-gauge (wrapping) wire. Insert one end of the wrapping wire from back to front through the second 1-in. (25.5 cm) curve on one end of the base, creating a short tail **(d)**. With the tail, make two snug wraps around the junction of the first and second curves, wrapping toward the small loop on this end of the base. Trim and tuck the tail wire (Basics, p. 109) **(e)**.

4 Make two more wraps with the remaining wire, wrapping away from the small loop and toward the nearest edge of the base. End with the wire on the top surface of the base.

5 String a 6 mm pearl **(f)**, and make two wraps around the junction of the next two curves **(g)**. Make sure you are wrapping in the same direction as before—toward the nearest edge. Repeat this step five more times.

6 To begin wrapping the other edge of the base, work as in steps 3–5, but in step 3, make the first wraps around the junction of the small loop and the first 1-in. (25.5 mm) curve **(h)**.

7 Continue to add pearls, alternating edges of the base for consistent tension. Do not attach a pearl inside the ½-in. (13 mm) curves, as they will be used for the clasp **(i)**.

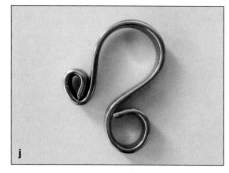

j

k

l

notes

- This aluminum wire is flat, 4 mm wide, and very pliable. I used a round pen as a mandrel to make the curves.
- Make a few practice curves with your pen or mandrel and 1 ft. (30.5 cm) of flat wire first.
- If needed, manipulate the flat wire with nylon-jaw pliers so you won't scratch the surface.
- Do not reshape or rework the flat wire too much.

Clasp

8 Flush-cut a 2½-in. (64 mm) piece of flat wire. Using roundnose pliers, make a small (4 mm) loop at one end. About ½ in. (13 mm) from the loop, make a curve, and then make a large (8 mm) loop on the other end **(j)**. The large loop needs to be large enough to attach to the first ½-in. (13 mm) curve of the base. The hook needs to be able to attach to the last ½-in. (13 mm) curve of the base.

9 Using roundnose pliers, unroll the large loop, attach the first ½-in. (13 mm) curve of the base, and roll the large loop closed again.

10 Cut a 6-in. (15.2 cm) piece of wrapping wire, and wrap the large loop of the clasp to the hook part of the clasp to close the loop and secure the bracelet **(k)**.

11 Carefully bend the bracelet into shape **(l)**. Try it on, and adjust the shape if necessary.

Wrapped & seeded bracelet

Keep it simple or make it fancy!
Transform two gauges of wire
into a dramatic, colorful, and fully
customizable bracelet.

by Lisa Niven Kelly

materials

Bracelet, custom diameter
- Copper practice wire, round, dead soft (optional):
  1 ft. (30.5 cm) 16-gauge (1.3 mm)
  10 ft. (3.1 m) 24-gauge (0.5 mm)
- Sterling silver wire, round, dead soft:
  1 ft. (30.5 cm) 16-gauge (1.3 mm)
  10 ft. (3.1 m) 24-gauge (0.5 mm)
- 15º seed beads in **3–5** colors (If you plan to patinate your bracelet, don't use dyed seed beads that will lose their color in water or liver of sulfur.)
- 16 mm swivel lobster claw clasp

tools & supplies
- Wirework toolbox, p. 105
- Flush cutters strong enough to cut 16-gauge (1.3 mm) wire
- Liver of sulfur with a Pro-Polish Pad, or 0000 steel wool and a polishing cloth (optional)

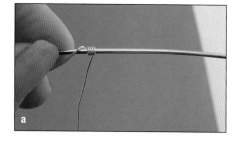

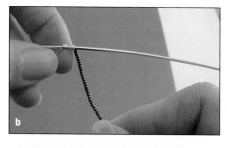

Practice

Practice coiling (Basics, p. 109) 24-gauge copper wire around 16-gauge copper wire before you use silver wire. Make the wraps nice and close to each other.

Next, string 3 in. (76 mm) of 15º seed beads onto the 24-gauge wire. Pinch the 24-gauge wire behind the beads as you coil them around the 16-gauge wire. (Don't pinch the beads too tightly, though, or they won't have room to spread slightly as you coil them.) Try to get the beads to coil evenly with no large gaps between them. The beads need to separate slightly to properly coil around the wire, but they shouldn't expose large amounts of the coiling wire. Practice until you feel comfortable with coiling.

Beaded core wire

1 Flush-cut a piece of 16-gauge sterling silver (core) wire 2 in. (51 mm) longer than the circumference of your wrist. This accounts for the amount of wire needed to form the loops for the clasp, and also allows the bracelet to move comfortably on your wrist.

2 Cut 1½ yd. (1.4 m) of 24-gauge sterling silver (coiling) wire. Fold it in half, and place the fold on the center of the core wire. Make four or five wraps around the center of the core wire **(a)**.

TIP
The initial wraps can slide on the core wire, so it's not necessary to wrap the core wire at the exact center just yet.

3 String approximately 2 in. (51 mm) of the first color of 15º seed beads onto the coiling wire **(b)**, and coil them onto the core wire. Make sure the coiling wire isn't exposed between beads.

4 After you've coiled the seed beads around the core wire, coil the coiling wire two to 10 times around the core wire to achieve the desired space between beaded coils **(c)**.

5 Repeat steps 3 and 4, changing bead colors as desired. Stop coiling when there's ¾ in. (19 mm) of the core wire exposed at the end.

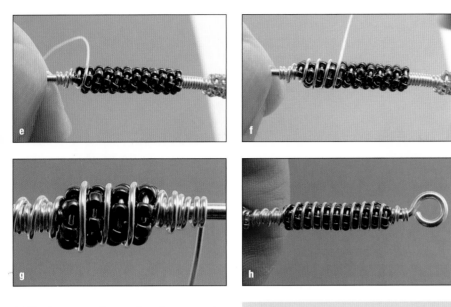

6 Flip the core wire so that the second half of the core wire extends to the right. Repeat steps 3–5 to coil around the exposed core wire with the second half of the coiling wire.

Trim and tuck the coiling wire (Basics, p. 109) on each end.

Overlay wire

7 Cut 1½ yd. (1.4 m) of 24-gauge (overlay) wire. Wrap the end of this wire twice around one end of the exposed core wire **(d)**.

8 Begin wrapping the overlay wire around the plain section of coiling, leaving approximately 2 mm between wraps **(e)**. Make sure to wrap the overlay wire in the same direction as the beaded coil. When you reach the first beaded coil, wrap the overlay wire around the beads, resting it in the grooves between wraps **(f)**.

Repeat this step to wrap the length of the core wire.

TIP

Don't wrap the overlay wire too tightly or the wire will slip down between the wraps of the beaded coil and you won't be able to see it. Think of "laying" the wire between the grooves rather than tightly wrapping it.

How many seed beads should I string?

- 1 in. (25.5 mm) beads = ¼ in. (6.5 mm) beaded coil (blue)
- 2 in. (51 mm) beads = ½ in. (13 mm) beaded coil (red)
- 3 in. (76 mm) beads = ¾ in. (19 mm) beaded coil (green)

9 When you reach the end of the core wire, wrap the overlay wire twice around the core wire **(g)**. Don't trim the tails.

TIP

Leave the tails in case you need to fill in some space after you make loops for the clasp.

Clasp

10 Make a plain loop (Basics, p. 109) with the exposed core wire on each end of the bracelet **(h)**, making a small loop on one end to attach the clasp, and a larger loop on the opposite end for the clasp to hook into.

If necessary, use the overlay wire tails to fill in any space between the loops and the coiling. Trim and tuck the tails.

11 Open the small plain loop (Basics, p. 109). Attach a swivel lobster claw clasp, and close the loop.

Finishing

12 Use your hands to begin to form the bracelet into a circle. Bring together the two ends of the bracelet, and hook the clasp into the large loop. Continue to form the bracelet into a circle.

13 If desired, patinate the bracelet with liver of sulfur (Basics, p. 110). Rinse the bracelet well, and let it dry. Use a Pro-Polish Pad or 0000 steel wool followed by a polishing cloth to remove the patina on the high points of the silver, leaving it dark in the recessed areas.

Design variation

Here are some suggestions for how to add further dimension and texture to your bracelet:

Coiled wrap

Cut 33 in. (83.8 cm) of 24-gauge sterling silver wire. Coil the wire tightly around a scrap piece of 18-gauge wire, making sure there are no gaps between the wraps. After you've made an approximately 4-in. (10.2 cm) coil, remove the coil from the scrap wire, and string it onto your coiling wire.

Wrap the coil around the core wire **(1)**. When you run out of coil, wrap the coiling wire directly around the core wire **(2)**. If desired, add an overlay wire just as you did over the seed beads.

> ## Note
> Learn how to coil wire with a drill by watching Lisa's free video tutorial at www.beaducation.com/vids/detail/156. The technique takes practice, but once mastered, it makes coiling much faster and easier.

Bead-and-coil wrap

String 2 in. (51 mm) of 15º seed beads onto the coiling wire, and coil them around the core wire **(3)**. Spread out the beaded coil so that there is an approximately 2 mm gap between the wraps **(4)**. When you add the overlay wire, string a 2-in. (51 mm) coil onto the wire, and wrap the coil into the gaps between the wraps of the beaded coil **(5)**.

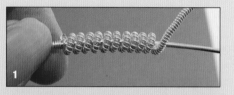

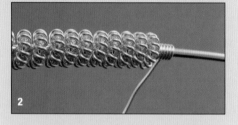

Dimensional wrap

String a 2-in. (51 mm) coil onto the coiling wire, and wrap the coil around the core wire. Spread out the coil so that there is an approximately 1 mm gap between the wraps. When you add the overlay wire, string 4½ in. (11.4 cm) of seed beads when you reach the coil. Wrap the beads into the gaps between the wraps of the coil **(6)**.

> ## Note
> I left a smaller gap between the coil wraps so the beads would sit up higher on the coil, rather than sink in between the wraps.

Metallic glam bangle

Turn simple charm bracelets into a grown-up bangle cuff that isn't afraid to shimmy, sparkle, and catch your eye. This shimmering wall of faceted beads and shining silver is finished with a chain and a briolette fringe for movement and style.

by Gretchen McHale

materials

small bracelet 6½ in. (16.5 cm);
medium bracelet 8 in. (20.3 cm)
- Sterling silver wire, round, dead-soft:
- 20-gauge (0.81 mm), 5 ft. (1.5 m)
- 24-gauge (0.51 mm), 8.5 ft. (2.6 m)
- Faceted Czech glass metallic
  rondelle beads
- **75** 4 mm
- **5** 2 mm
- **32** top-drilled, faceted onion-cut
  beads
- **4** 16-loop bangles
- **2** yd. (1.8 m) assorted chains

tools & supplies
- Wirework toolbox, p. 105

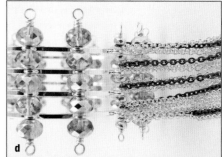

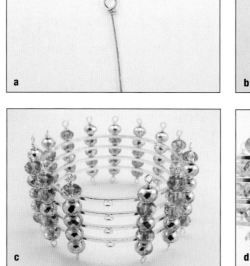

1 Cut 15 4-in. (10.2 cm) pieces of 20-gauge (0.81 mm) sterling silver wire. Make a small wrapped loop (Basics, p. 109) on one end of each wire **(a)**.

2 On one wire, string a 4 mm rondelle, a loop of a bangle, a 4 mm rondelle, a bangle loop, a 4 mm rondelle, a bangle loop, a 4 mm rondelle, a bangle loop, and a 4 mm rondelle. Make a small wrapped loop at the top of the stacked unit **(b)**.

3 Repeat step 2 with the remaining wires. One set of bangle loops will be unused **(c)**.

4 Cut assorted chains into 20 pieces of various lengths.

5 Cut a 4-in. (10.2 cm) piece of 24-gauge (0.51 mm) sterling silver wire, and make a wrapped loop on one end. On the wire, string a 2 mm rondelle, the top links of four chains, and the bottom unused bangle loop. After each bangle loop, string the top link of four chains and a 2 mm rondelle. Make a small wrapped loop at the top of the stacked unit **(d)**.

6 Cut 32 3-in. (76 mm) pieces of 24-gauge (0.51 mm) sterling silver wire. On one wire, string a top-drilled bead,

and make a set of wraps above it (Basics, p. 110) **(e)**. Make the first half of a wrapped loop above the wraps **(f)**. Repeat to make a total of 32 dangles.

7 Slide a dangle's loop through a top loop on a stacked unit, and finish the wraps. Repeat to attach a top-drilled dangle to each top and bottom loop of a stacked unit **(g)**.

Hinged frame cuff

Handmade hinges connect beaded frames (made from hardware cloth!) in this intricate cuff. Choose your favorite beads to customize your bracelet.

by Barb Switzer

materials

Bracelet 7½ in. (19.1 cm)

- Sterling silver wire, round, dead-soft:
- 16-gauge (1.29 mm), 18 in. (45.7 cm)
- 18-gauge (1.02 mm), 5 ft. (1.5 m)
- 30-gauge (0.26 mm), 16 ft. (4.9 m)
- 8 hardware-cloth frames: 1 x 2 in. (25.5 x 51 mm) (see "note," below)
- 32–40 6 mm beads
- 32–60 3–4 mm beads
- 32–50 4 mm daisy spacers
- 4–6 1–1.5 mm spacers (to string between clasp coils, optional)
- 3 g 8° cylinder beads
- Box clasp
- 2 jump rings: 18-gauge (1.02 mm), 4 mm inside diameter (optional)

tools & supplies

- Wirework toolbox, p. 105
- Three-step Master Coiler coiling pliers
- G-S Hypo Cement (optional)

note

The frames are cut from ½-in. (13 mm) hardware cloth, which is made of 19-gauge (0.91 mm) galvanized steel wire and comes in rolls from garden centers and hardware stores.

If you wish to cut your own frames, use a Dremel rotary hand tool with a fiberglass cutting blade to separate the pieces. Always use extreme caution, covering your eyes, nose, mouth, and exposed skin to prevent injury. You could also use heavy-duty shears or old cutters, but you'll need to file the edges after cutting. Do not use your good jewelry cutters on this material.

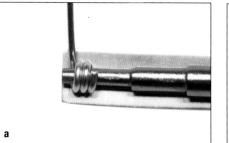

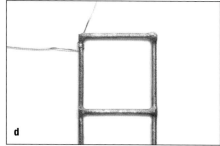

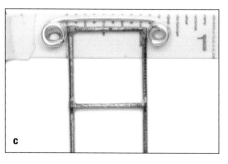

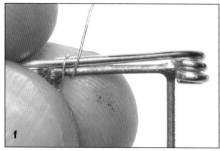

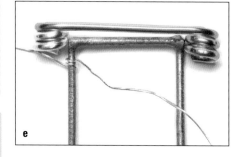

Hinge findings

1 Cut 16 2¾-in. (70 mm) pieces of 18-gauge (1.02 mm) wire, making sure both ends are cut flush.

TIP

Cut one piece and use it to measure the remaining pieces to the same exact length.

Using the smallest step of your coiling pliers, grasp the tip of one wire and turn the pliers to begin making a coil, rotating so the wire's tip goes toward the inside of the pliers. Make two-and-a-half wraps **(a)**.

2 Repeat on the other end of the wire, rotating so the wire's tip goes toward the tip of the pliers **(b)**. The two coils should face the same direction. Measure the wire between the coils; it should be 9/16 in. (14 mm), and a hardware-cloth frame should fit between the coils **(c)**. If the straight segment is too long or too short, adjust the coils as needed.

This hinge finding has two sides. The side with the straight span of wire is the front and the side that shows the wire ends is the back.

Repeat steps 1 and 2 to make a total of 16 hinge findings.

Frames

The hardware-cloth frames also have a front and back side. The side on which the short wires cross over the long wires will be on the front of the bracelet.

3 Center 24 in. (61 cm) of 30-gauge (0.26 mm) wrapping wire on one long side of a frame, and make two wraps **(d)**. Position a hinge finding along the adjacent short side of the frame so that the front of the hinge finding and the front of the frame are facing the same direction and the coils on the hinge finding face the center of the frame **(e)**.

Wrap around both the hinge finding and the frame, making 12–16 wraps across the frame **(f)**. Turn the corner, and wrap the long side, making six to eight wraps per square **(g, h)**.

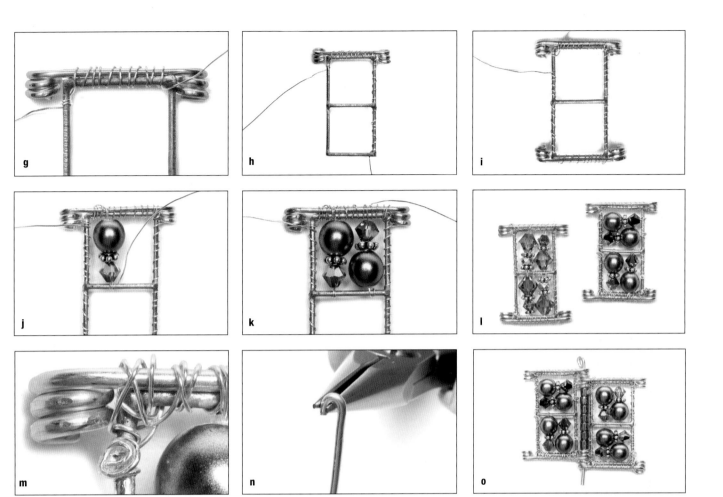

g

h

i

j

k

l

m

n

o

4 Using the same wrapping wire, repeat step 3 to position a hinge finding along the other short side and make wraps. Do not trim the wire tail **(i)**.

5 Using the tail from step 3, make a few wraps to reach one-third of the way down the frame's short edge. Slide 3–6 mm beads and spacers as desired (I used a 6 mm, a 4 mm daisy spacer, and a 4 mm) onto the wrapping wire. The beads should span the square, but to prevent them from buckling and popping out of the frame, allow a little wiggle room. Make one or two wraps around the opposite frame wire **(j)**. Thread the wire back through the beads.

6 Wrap the wire around the frame several times to create a gap before adding the next row. Using the same wrapping wire, repeat step 5, alternating the position of the beads as desired so the rows fit **(k)**.

7 Add two rows of beads in the remaining square, positioning them

either parallel or perpendicular to the beads in the first square **(l)**.

8 Make a few wraps around the frame, and trim the wrapping wire to ⅜ in. (9.5 mm). Using the wire tail, make a spiral (Basics, p. 109). Press the spiral against the frame, and glue it in place with a drop of G-S Hypo Cement **(m)**.

Alternatively, skip the spiral, and wrap the tail around the frame five or six times. Trim the end, and press it against the frame.

Repeat steps 3–8 with the remaining frames and hinge findings, varying the bead choice and placement as desired.

Assembly

9 To make a hinge pin, use flush cutters to cut a 1¾-in. (44 mm) piece of 16-gauge (1.29 mm) wire. Using chain-nose or flatnose pliers, grasp the wire about ⅛ in. (3 mm) from one end, and make a right-angle bend. Bend the short end of the wire into a hook, and use pliers to squeeze the hook closed **(n)**.

10 Align two frames so the hinge coils of one are stacked above the hinge coils of the other. Slide the hinge pin through the first two coils, seven 8º cylinder beads, and the remaining two coils **(o)**.

note
When you're threading the hinge pins to attach the frames, you can substitute sections of coiled wire for the 8º cylinder beads.

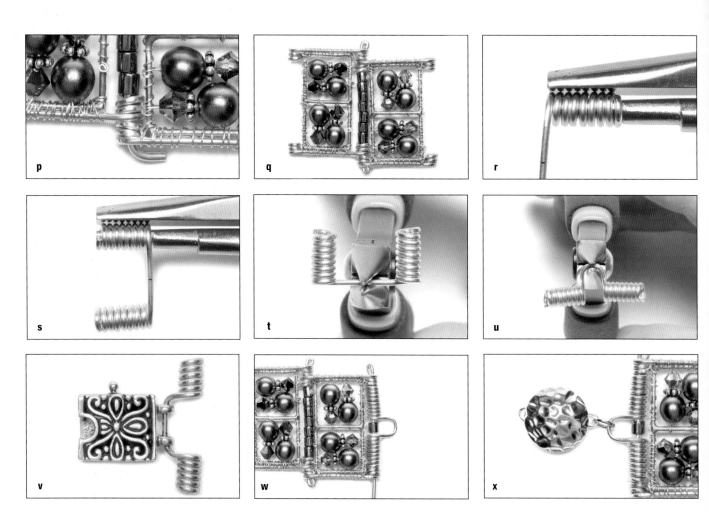

11 Grasp the hinge pin 1/16 in. (1.5 mm) from the last coil, and make a right-angle bend **(p)**. Leaving the space between the coil and the bend is essential; it allows the frames to move freely on their hinges. If necessary, trim the wire to 1/8 in. (3 mm) from the bend. Make a second hook **(q)**.

Repeat steps 9–11 to connect the remaining frames, attaching them in a zigzag pattern.

End components

12 Flush-cut 7½ in. (19.1 cm) of 18-gauge (1.02 mm) wire, and mark the center with a permanent marker. Using the smallest step of your coiling pliers and rotating so the wire's tip goes toward the inside of the pliers, make a coil that ends 3/16 in. (5 mm) from the center mark **(r)**.

If the loops on your box clasp are perpendicular to the clasp, string one half of the clasp on the wire now. (If the loops are parallel to the clasp, you can attach it after you've assembled both end components.)

On the other end of the wire, make another coil of the same length, coiling toward the tip of the pliers so the coils go in the same direction **(s)**. There should be 3/8 in. (9.5 mm) between the coils. If your coils aren't exactly the same length, trim the longer one to match the shorter one.

13 Using roundnose or coiling pliers, grasp the wire's center mark **(t)**. Bend each end down to make a U, and align the coils with each other **(u)**.

If you're using a two-strand clasp, you'll need to make a square bend **(v)**.

Repeat steps 12 and 13 to make a second end component.

14 Cut wire for a hinge pin and make the first hook. Slide the hinge pin through a coil on an end frame, an end component coil, one or more spacer beads or 8° cylinders, the remaining end component coil, and the remaining frame coil. Complete the second hook of the hinge pin **(w)**.

Repeat to attach the remaining end component to the other end of the bracelet.

15 If your box clasp loops are parallel with the clasp, open a 4 mm jump ring (Basics, p. 110), attach a U-bend and the clasp, and close the jump ring **(x)**. Repeat on the other end.

Loopy copper cuff

This looping technique creates a structural base with retro-modern style and is sure to spark new ideas and designs. Create a cuff or bangle that makes the perfect home for your favorite round bead.

by Hana Terpo

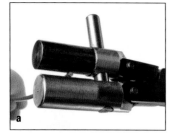
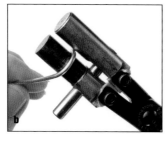

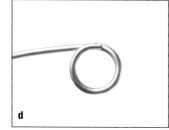

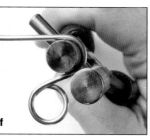
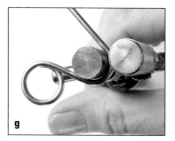

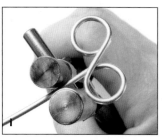

materials

- Round, dead-soft copper wire:
- 13 ft. (4 m), 14-gauge (1.6 mm)
- 4 ft. (1.25 m), 24-gauge (0.5 mm)
- **60** 8 mm round beads

tools & supplies

- Wirework toolbox, p. 105
- Bail-making pliers with an 8 mm jaw
- Bracelet mandrel or wrist-sized round object to use for shaping

note

The Swanstrom Parallel Action Bail-Forming pliers used in the photos are one of several types of bail-making pliers available. The large, 10 mm diameter jaw never changes, but the opposing jaw is interchangeable and comes with five size options. An 8 mm jaw is used in the photos. The project designer used Wubbers Large Bail-Making Pliers that have a small 6 mm diameter jaw opposite a large 8 mm jaw, forming the loops on the large jaw. In the photos, the 8 mm jaw is colored green and the 10 mm jaw is referred to as the opposing jaw in text. If you use Wubbers Large Bail-Making Pliers, the opposing jaw will be smaller, instead of larger like the tool in the photos.

TIP

Before starting, make several test loops with a 15-in. (38.1 cm) piece of wire to get a feel for the heavy wire and to practice the technique.

1 Work directly from a spool or a coil of 14-gauge (1.6 mm) wire at least 8 ft. (2.5 m) long. Flush cut the end of the wire. Place the 8 mm jaw (green) of the bail-making pliers on top and as close as possible to the wire end and close the jaws of the pliers to grasp the wire firmly **(a)**.

2 Begin to form a loop around the 8 mm jaw by rotating the pliers 90 degrees away from your body **(b)**. Open the jaw and roll the opposing (brass) jaw back up toward the ceiling **(c)**. Finish shaping a loop by overlapping the wire end, wrapping it toward the pliers' handles **(d)**.

3 Position the 8mm jaw above the wire and the opposing jaw next to the loop **(e)**. Use your non-dominant hand to pull the wire halfway around the 8 mm jaw **(f)**. Pivot the pliers 90 degrees, rotating the opposing jaw away from the middle of the forming pair of loops **(g)**. Pull the wire around the 8 mm jaw on the side closest to the handles until it creates a complete loop and points directly away from the forming row of loops **(h)**. The resulting shape is a slightly off-center figure-8.

4 Position the 8 mm jaw above the wire and the opposing jaw next to the previous loop **(i)**. Pull the wire around the 8mm jaw, beginning a second loop **(j)**. Pull the wire around in front of the center wire, toward the tip of the pliers, to complete a second loop **(k)**. When making loops on first side (with the overlapped end), pull the wire around toward the tip of the pliers. When making loops on the second side, pull the wire around toward the handle of the pliers. Pay close attention to this orientation while forming loops, and be consistent.

l

m

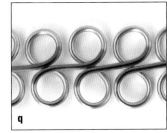

n

o

p

q

r

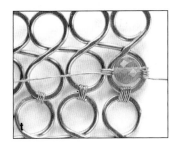

s

t

5 Position the 8 mm jaw above the wire and the opposing jaw next to the loop you just created **(l)**. Pull the wire around the 8 mm jaw to begin making another loop. Reposition the opposing jaw to the outside of the loop and finish pulling the wire around toward the handles of the pliers to finish the loop **(m)**.

TIP

Leave at least a 1–1.5 mm (1/16 in.) gap between each row of loops to leave room for the wire to spread when the strip is hammered.

6 For an open, slip-on cuff with no clasp, make the strip ¼ in. (6.5 mm) longer than your wrist measurement **(n)**. To make a bangle that slides on over your hand, measure your hand around the widest part, and add ½ in. (13 mm) to the measurement.

7 Flush cut the wire on the last loop so the wire end is not visible from the front side of the strip. File the end so that it overlaps and tucks neatly onto the inside of the cuff without scratching your skin **(o)**. Repeat steps 1–7 to make a second loopy strip.

8 The top side of the strip has a wire crossing the middle, a gap, and then another wire crossing the middle **(p)**. The bottom side of the strip has two wires that sit next to each other down the center between the two loops **(q)**.

9 Place a loopy strip on a steel bench block. With the bottom side facing up, start by tapping lightly down the center of the whole strip using a chasing hammer. Next, begin to hammer the loops flat **(r)**. Hammer one loop, then switch to the loop on the opposite side, continuing down the whole length of the strip until all loops are flattened.

10 Set the strips side-by-side arranged mirror-image to each other. Working off of a long coil or spool of wire, start at the center of the strips, and connect two corresponding loops by wrapping three or four times with 24-gauge (0.5 mm) wire **(s)**. Next, wrap together the end loops in the same manner to connect the pieces securely. Continue wrapping until all of the corresponding loops are

attached. Because the loopy strips are not perfectly straight along the side, some of the loops may overlap slightly.

TIP

Choose beads slightly smaller than the inner diameter to leave room for wire used to attach the beads to the frame.

11 Cut a piece of 24-gauge (0.5 mm) wire roughly three times the length of the bracelet. Starting on one end of the frame, attach the wire to the first loop by wrapping it three or four times. Pull the wire across the front side of the strip and string a bead. Wrap around both of the next two adjacent loops two or three times **(t)**. Continue down the length of the bracelet.

Repeat on the remaining rows of loops using a new piece of wire for each row. At the end of each row, wrap the wire several times around the loop, trim the wire and tuck the end against the bottom of the loopy strip using chainnose pliers.

u

12 Start on one end of the bracelet and gradually bend it into a curved shape around a mandrel or round object. Repeat on the opposite end to begin shaping the curve. Next, push the middle against a bracelet mandrel to continue to curve the shape. Apply pressure with your fingers and move any loops that are slightly out of place. Reshape until the bracelet fits well, and is easy to put on and take off **(u)**.

13 If desired, apply liver of sulfur to add a patina. Use a brass brush to highlight and polish the exposed areas to add contrast. If there is any chance that the patina solution will stain or discolor the beads chosen for the design, patina the frame and 24-gauge (0.5 mm) wrapping wire before adding beads.

The looping technique can be done on any size pliers, using different gauges of wire.

The loops of this delicate bangle are made from 18-gauge sterling wire looped around the largest part of the jaw of conventional roundnose pliers. The frame is filled with 4 mm beads. The strip is long and overlaps to create a four-row centerpiece on the bangle. A single additional loop centered on both ends provides a scrolled decorative finish.

To make a narrower cuff, complete one loopy strip, add beads and shape the cuff. For a narrower cuff, make the strip longer and wrap the ends together. This example is made with 6 mm beads.

Wrapped barbell bracelet

Build sturdy wrapped links and attach them with wire figure-8s. This attractive design makes great necklaces or bracelets for men or women, and you can choose copper, silver-filled, or other sterling alternatives for economical gift giving.

by Barb Switzer

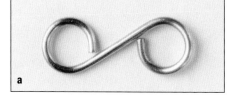

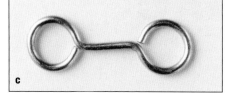

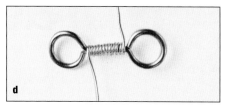

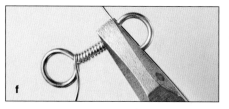

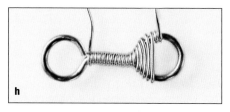

materials

Bracelet 6¾–8 in. (17.1–20.3 cm)

- Copper, sterling silver, or silver-filled wire, round, dead soft:
  - 24–28 in. (61.0–71.1 cm) 18-gauge (1.0 mm)
  - 9–10½ ft. (2.7–3.2 m) 24-gauge (0.5 mm)

tools & supplies

- Wirework toolbox, p. 105
- Large roundnose pliers (jaws must be at least 5 mm in diameter)
- Liver of sulfur (optional)
- Steel wool (optional)
- Tumbler with steel shot (optional)

Barbell links

1 Flush-cut both ends of a 1⅝-in. (41 mm) piece of 18-gauge wire. Using large roundnose pliers, grasp one end of the wire where the jaw is 5 mm in diameter, and roll the pliers to make a loop. Repeat on the other end of the wire, rolling in the opposite direction **(a)**.

2 Use the tip of your chainnose pliers to grasp just inside one loop, and make a 90-degree bend **(b)**. Repeat on the other loop.

3 Position the jaws of the chainnose pliers between the loops. Close the jaws, squeezing the wire straight between the loops. Close the loops as tightly as possible. The wire will be shaped like a barbell **(c)**.

4 Cut an 18-in. (45.7 cm) piece of 24-gauge wire. Center the wire on the straight part of the barbell. Using each half of the wire, wrap around the straight part of the barbell until it's entirely covered **(d)**.

TIP

Resist the temptation to use nylon-jaw pliers to straighten the 24-gauge wrapping wire; doing so will harden the wire, making it difficult to finish wrapping around the loop of the link without breaking the wire.

5 With one end of the wire, wrap around the base of the loop four times **(e)**. Using flatnose pliers, squeeze gently to flatten the wire against the loop **(f)**. Do not use too much force; the idea is to flatten the wire without smashing or marring it.

6 Wrap three more times around the loop, keeping each wrap tight against the previous wrap **(g)**. Gently squeeze the wire flat after each full wrap. After completing the wraps, use flatnose pliers to squeeze the wire against one side of the loop.

7 Feed the wire through the loop, and wrap the wire around one side **(h)**. Do not pull too hard, and avoid opening the loop or distorting the shape of the barbell.

8 Cut a scrap of polishing pad, and fold it in half around the loop, leaving the last wraps visible. Using flatnose pliers, hold the straight section of the barbell and the portion of the loop that's already been wrapped. The pad prevents marring and holds everything in place during wrapping. Continue wrapping the wire around the loop until there is room for only one more wrap **(i)**. Pull the wire down through the loop and up against the inside of the loop. Trim the end as close to the loop as possible. Use chainnose pliers to squeeze the end of the wire and tuck it inside the loop.

9 Repeat steps 5–8 on the other loop **(j)**. Make a total of six or seven barbell links.

i

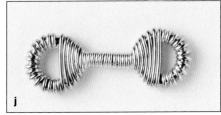

j

k

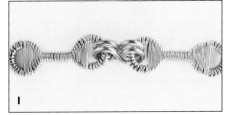

l

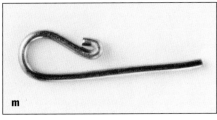

m

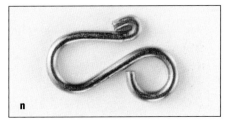

n

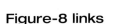

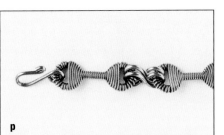

o

p

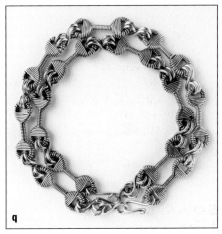

q

Figure-8 links

10 Flush-cut both ends of a 1-in. (25.5 mm) piece of 18-gauge wire. Using roundnose pliers, grasp one end of the wire where the jaw is about 3.5 mm in diameter, and roll the pliers to make a loop. Repeat on the other end, rolling in the opposite direction **(k)**. Make a total of 13 figure-8 links for a bracelet with six barbell links, or make a total of 15 figure-8 links for a bracelet with seven barbell links.

11 Open one loop of a figure-8 link, attach a barbell link, and close the figure-8 link. Attach a second figure-8 link next to the previous one. Open both remaining loops of the figure-8 links, attach a second barbell link, and close both loops **(l)**. Repeat to attach all the barbell links with pairs of figure-8 links.

On one end of the chain, end with two figure-8 links. On the other end of the chain, end with a barbell link. You will have one figure-8 link left over.

Clasp

12 Flush-cut both ends of a 1¼-in. (32 mm) piece of 18-gauge wire. Using chainnose or flatnose pliers, grasp one end, and pull it around to form a folded end. Position your roundnose pliers near the folded end, and pull the wire around the jaw of the pliers to form a hook **(m)**. Make a loop on the other end of the wire that sits slightly underneath the hook **(n)**.

13 Open one loop of the remaining figure-8 link, attach the two figure-8 links on one end of the bracelet, and close the loop **(o)**. Open the loop of the hook, attach the barbell link on the other end of the bracelet, and close the loop **(p)**.

14 If desired, patinate the bracelet with liver of sulfur (Basics, p. 110), polish with steel wool or a polishing pad, and tumble with steel shot (Basics, p. 110) to enhance the shine and contrast **(q)**.

NECKLACES
&
PENDANTS

Just-after-sunset necklace

Natural stones work together with antiqued copper wire to give this necklace an earthy, yet ethereal feel.

by Zoraida Bros

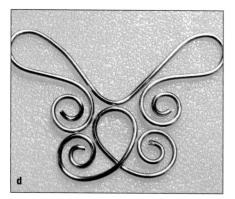

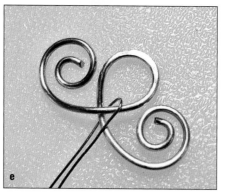

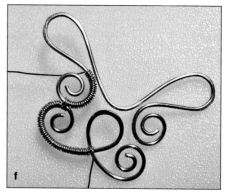

materials

Necklace 20½ in. (52.1 cm)

- Copper wire, round, dead soft:
  - 25 in. (63.5 cm) 16-gauge (1.3 mm)
  - 4 in. (10.2 cm) 18-gauge (1.0 mm)
  - 40 in. (1 m) 20-gauge (0.8 mm)
  - 4 ft. (1.2 m) 24-gauge (0.5 mm)
- **1** large top-drilled pendant (agate)
- **8** 12–14 mm round beads (ocean jasper)
- **10** 10–12 mm rondelles or round beads (pink rose quartz)

tools & supplies

- Wirework toolbox, p. 105
- Flush cutters strong enough to cut 16-gauge (1.3 mm) wire
- Looping pliers with ½-in. (13 mm) jaw, ½-in. (13 mm) dowel, or other cylindrical object
- Liver of sulfur (optional)

TIP

The hole in the pendant must be large enough to accommodate 18-gauge wire. The other bead holes must be able to accommodate 20-gauge wire.

Pendant hanger

1 Flush-cut an 8-in. (20.3 cm) piece of 16-gauge wire. On each end, form an open spiral (Basics, p. 109) about ½ in. (13 mm) in diameter with the spirals facing the same direction.

2 Using the ½-in. (13 mm) jaw of looping pliers, a ½-in. (13 mm) dowel, or other cylindrical object, bend the wire at its midpoint so that the spirals face each other **(a)**.

3 Locate the midpoint between the bend and the spiral on one side, and bend the wire outward. Repeat for the other side. With the spirals facing outward, continue bending the wire until the spirals are ½ in. (13 mm) apart **(b)**.

4 Flush-cut a 5-in. (12.7 cm) piece of 16-gauge wire. On each end, form an open spiral as in step 1.

5 Repeat step 2, and continue bending the wire until it crosses itself and the spirals face outward **(c)**.

6 Position this hanger piece so that the loop and spirals are facing up. Position the first hanger piece above it, so the loop of the bottom hanger piece sits between the spirals of the top hanger piece **(d)**. Adjust any of the spirals or loops if necessary.

7 Place the hanger pieces on an anvil. Using a chasing hammer, hammer the two loops of the top hanger piece and the center loop of the bottom hanger piece. Only hammer small sections at a time so the hanger pieces keep their shape and continue to fit together properly. Do not hammer where the wires cross in the bottom hanger piece, and do not hammer any of the spirals.

8 Cut 1 yd. (91.4 cm) of 24-gauge (wrapping) wire, fold it in half, and slide it through the center loop of the bottom hanger piece **(e)**.

9 With one half of the wrapping wire, wrap around the left side of the bottom hanger piece until you reach the place where the left spiral meets the left spiral

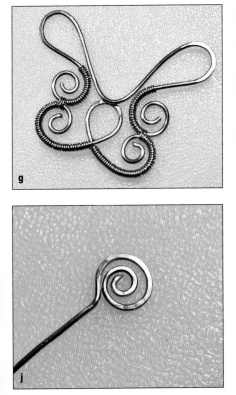

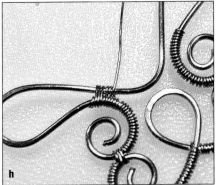

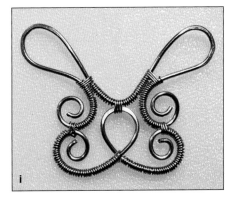

of the top hanger piece. Make three wraps around both spirals, ending with your wire pointing toward the top hanger piece. Continue wrapping around the top hanger piece until you reach the place where the left spiral and left loop meet **(f)**. Trim and tuck this half of the wrapping wire (Basics, p. 109).

10 With the remaining half of the wrapping wire, repeat step 9 for the right side of the hanger pieces **(g)**.

11 Cut a 12-in. (30.5 cm) piece of wrapping wire. Leaving a 1-in. (25.5 mm) tail, make one wrap around the bottom arm of the top hanger piece about ⅛ in. (3 mm) from the previous wraps on the left side.

TIP

The space will be tight, so hold the hanger pieces firmly in your non-dominant hand for better control.

Make three or four wraps around both arms of the left loop, filling the space between the first wrap made in this step and the previous wraps. Continue wrapping around just the top arm of the loop as you move toward the center of the top hanger piece **(h)**.

12 Make three or four wraps around both the top hanger piece and the center loop of the bottom hanger piece.

13 Begin wrapping around just the top arm of the right loop until your wraps are even with those of the previously wrapped spiral. Make three wraps around both arms of the right loop, and wrap once around just the bottom arm. Trim and tuck the wire as before **(i)**.

Pendant

14 Flush-cut a 4-in. (10.2 cm) piece of 18-gauge wire. On one end, form an open spiral about ½ in. (13 mm) in diameter. Using the chasing hammer and anvil, slightly hammer the spiral **(j)**. Do not hammer the stem of the wire.

15 With the stem of the wire, form a hook slightly above the end of the spiral **(k)**. Insert the stem through the pendant from back to front with the spiral facing the front of the pendant. Bend the stem up toward the top of the pendant, and continue around the back of the stem to form a small hook. Trim any excess wire **(l)**.

16 Slide the spiral through the center loop of the bottom hanger piece from back to front.

TIP

It may be necessary to slide the spiral through the loop sideways if the spiral is large.

With your fingers, press the spiral in toward the pendant to close the gap. Adjust the spiral so your pendant is able to swing **(m)**.

Beaded chains

17 Cut a 1¼-in. (32 mm) piece of 20-gauge wire, and make a plain loop (Basics, p. 109) on one end. String a 12–14 mm round bead, and make another plain loop. Repeat to make three more round-bead units.

18 Cut a 3-in. (76 mm) piece of 20-gauge wire, and make the first half of a wrapped loop (Basics, p. 109). String a 10–12 mm rondelle right up to the loop (do not leave room for wraps), and make the first half of a wrapped loop against the other end of the rondelle. Spiral the remaining wire tails around the ends of the rondelle. Repeat to make three more rondelle units.

m

n

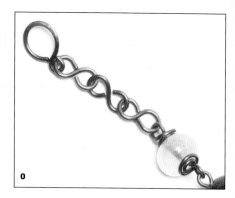

o

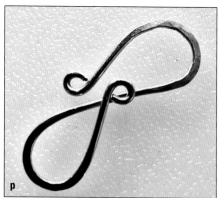

p

TIP

You can make plain loops instead of the spiraled loops in step 18. To do so, cut just ¾ in. (19 mm) of 20-gauge wire.

19 Open the plain loops (Basics, p. 109) of the round-bead units, and attach the loops of the rondelle units to make a beaded chain of alternating round beads and rondelles **(n)**.

20 Make one more rondelle unit as in step 18, but before forming the spiral on each end, attach one loop to one side of the pendant hanger, and attach the other loop to the round-bead unit at one end of the beaded chain. Complete the spirals.

TIP

If desired, a small jump ring may be used to attach the rondelle unit to the pendant hanger.

21 Repeat steps 17–20 to make the other beaded chain.

Figure-8 links

22 Flush-cut a 1¼-in. (32 mm) piece of 16-gauge wire. With roundnose pliers, grasp one end of the wire, and roll it toward the center. Grasp the other end

of the wire, and roll it the opposite way. Adjust the loops to create a figure-8 link. Make five more figure-8 links.

23 Open the loops of the links, and attach three links to the end of each beaded chain.

Hook-and-eye clasp

24 For the eye: Flush-cut a 1½-in. (38 mm) piece of 16-gauge wire. Form a figure-8 link, but make one loop smaller than the other. With the chasing hammer and anvil, slightly hammer the loops. Attach the smaller loop to the figure-8 link at one end of the necklace **(o)**.

25 For the hook: Flush-cut a 3-in. (76 mm) piece of 16-gauge wire. Leaving the center 1 in. (25.5 mm) straight, make a bend at each end of the wire, pulling the wire in opposite directions. Using roundnose pliers, make a small loop at each end of the wire, with the loops facing outward. With the chasing hammer and anvil, slightly hammer the bends in the wire **(p)**. Attach the hook to the figure-8 link at the remaining end of the necklace.

TIP

Using your fingers or pliers, bend the end of the loop that is attached to the figure-8 link so that it overlaps the center of the hook for a more secure hold **(p)**.

26 Check all links, making sure they are closed tight. Use a needle file if necessary to smooth any sharp edges. If desired, patinate the necklace with liver of sulfur (Basics, p. 110), making sure your pendant and beads are not delicate or porous, as they may discolor.

Tangled squares necklace

Create components with an overlapping, organic wrapping technique. Lampworked beads add a sophisticated dimension, and a patina highlights the texture and layers in this celebration of hand-built beauty.

by Lisa Liddy

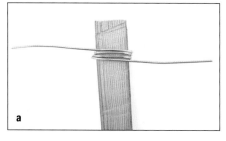

a

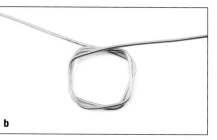

b

c

a

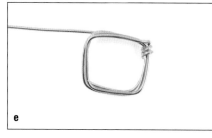

e

f

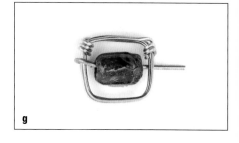

g

materials

necklace 19 in. (48.3 cm)

- Copper wire, round, dead-soft:
- 14-gauge (1.63 mm), 4 in. (10.2 cm)
- 16-gauge (1.29 mm), 8 in. (20.3 cm)
- 18-gauge (1.0 mm), 17½ ft. (5.3 m)
- **18** 8 mm copper jump rings, 14-gauge (1.63 mm)
- **3** 12 mm lampworked barrel-shaped beads
- **4** 6 x 12 mm lampworked disk beads

tools & supplies

- Wirework toolbox, p. 105
- liver of sulfur gel
- fine-grade steel wool

1 Measure and cut 19 11-in. (27.9 cm) pieces of 18-gauge (1.02 mm) wire.

2 Leaving a 1½-in. (38 mm) tail on the starting end, wrap one 18-gauge (1.02 mm) wire around a 15 mm square mandrel **(a)**. Wrap the wire three-and-a-quarter times around the mandrel so the ending tail of the wire is on the corner opposite the starting end, but on the same side of the mandrel **(b)**. As you wrap, bend the corners as close as possible to 90 degrees.

3 Slide the wrapped wire square off the mandrel. Use flatnose pliers to hold the square on the side with the loose ends so that all wires are together **(c)**.

4 Using chainnose pliers, wrap one tail tightly around all three wires at the corner three times **(d)**. Wrap until the end of the tail is inside the square. Trim any excess and make sure the wire end is tucked inside the square **(e)**. Repeat to wrap the other tail **(f)**. The resulting wrapped square may no longer be even and strands might overlap. It is fine if some squares come out with the wrapped ends on the same corner or

do not match perfectly, since the goal is to create organic links.

5 Repeat steps 2–4 to create 18 more wrapped squares.

note

The necklace in this project is 19 in. (48.3 cm) long. To adjust your necklace's length, just add or subtract wrapped squares.

6 Cut five 1⁹⁄₁₆-in. (40 mm) pieces of 16-gauge (1.29 mm) wire. Take one finished square, a piece of 16-gauge (1.29 mm) wire, and one barrel-shaped lampworked bead. Using roundnose pliers, make a plain loop (Basics, p. 109) on one end of the wire. Open the loop using chainnose pliers. Slide one side of

h

i

j

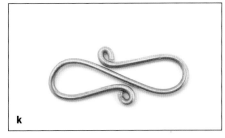

k

l

m

a wrapped square into the loop, and close it. String the bead onto the wire **(g)**. With the roundnose pliers, form another loop around the opposite side of the wrapped square **(h)**. Try to position your loop as close as possible to the bead **(i)**.

7 Using the 16-gauge (1.29 mm) wire pieces, make two more components with barrel-shaped beads following instructions in step 6. Repeat twice with two disk-shaped lampworked beads.

8 Open 18 14-gauge (1.63 mm) 8 mm jump rings. Slide two of the wrapped squares without beads onto a jump ring, then close the ring **(j)**. Continue adding squares and jump rings in this order: three plain squares, one square with stacked disk beads, one plain square, one barrel-bead square, one plain square, one barrel-bead square, one plain square, one barrel-bead square, one plain square, one square with stacked disk beads, four plain squares.

note
Don't worry too much about making the links match one another perfectly. The intent is to allow for a little variation to give the finished necklace a more organic feel.

9 With flush cutters, cut a 4-in. (10.2 cm) piece of 14-gauge (1.63 mm) copper wire. Use roundnose pliers to make a very small loop on each end. Shape the wire into an S using large roundnose pliers **(k)**. Place the S on a bench block, and use a chasing hammer to flatten the wire. Use the peen of the chasing hammer to texture the clasp **(l)**.

10 Open one end of the clasp, and slip it through one of the tangled square ends. Close the clasp. Use the square on the other end as the closure **(m)**.

11 Finish the necklace by adding a patina using liver of sulfur. After patinating, allow the necklace to dry, and then use fine-grade steel wool to polish and bring out the highlights of the copper.

Flower pendant

Transform a classic wrought-iron design into a modern and wearable flower pendant. Fine tune your spirals and weave them together to form a sturdy, beautiful structure.

by Lisa Niven Kelly

materials

Pendant 1½ x 1½ in. (38 x 38 mm)

- Sterling silver-filled, dead soft, round wire:
  - 2 ft. (61 cm) 18-gauge (1.0 mm)
  - 5 ft. (1.5 m), 28-gauge (0.32 mm)
- **1** jump ring, 18-gauge (1.0 mm), 4 mm inner diameter (ID)

tools & supplies

Wirework toolbox, p. 105

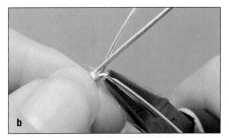

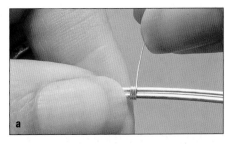

1 Cut three 7-in. (17.8 cm) pieces of 18-gauge (1.0 mm) wire. Cut a 3 ft. (91.4 cm) piece of 28-gauge (0.32 mm) wire. Hold the first 2 in. (51 mm) of 28-gauge (0.32 mm) in your non-dominant hand. Wrap four times very tightly around the center of the 18-gauge wires to bind the 18-gauge (1.0 mm) wires into a triangular bundle **(a)**. Do not cut away the 28-gauge wire at either end of the coil.

2 Using the tip of your chainnose pliers, grab one of the 18-gauge wires just above the end of the coil, and bend it into to a 90-degree angle **(b)**. Repeat this angle on the same wire on the bottom side of the four wraps. Repeat on another piece of 18-gauge wire **(c)**, leaving the third wire straight to create an armature with six equally-spaced legs protruding from the coil **(d)**.

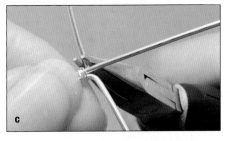

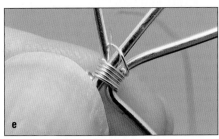

3 Wrap the long length of the 28-gauge wire over two of the legs **(e)** and around the second leg. Continue counterclockwise, crossing over and then wrapping around the next leg over **(f)**. Continue to wrap around each leg one time all the way around the armature **(g)**.

TIP

Do not worry if some sections are wider or narrower than others.

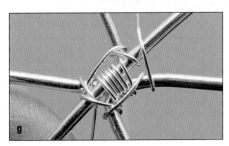

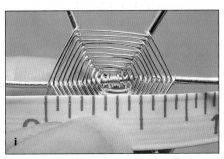

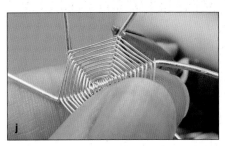

4 Continue the same wrapping pattern with similar tension around the armature **(h)**. Weave until the widest sections measure ⅜ in. (9.5 mm) from the center **(i)**. End the wire by coiling it once or twice around the closest leg, trimming off the wire and tucking down the end with chainnose pliers. Wrap the 2-in.

(51 mm) tail wire once or twice and trim off the remaining wire.

5 Measuring from the woven section of the armature out toward the ends, trim each 18-gauge (1.0 mm) leg to 1¾ in. (44 mm). Using the tip of your chainnose pliers, bend each leg sideways, in the same direction, to slightly less than a 45-degree angle **(j)**.

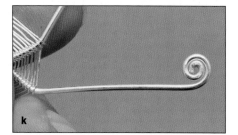

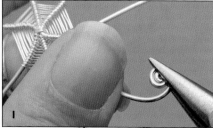

6 At the end of each wire leg, form a spiral (Basics, p. 109). Start with a closed, tight spiral just under two rotations **(k)**. Continue to form the spiral, allowing it to open up as it rolls toward the next leg over **(l)**. Stop when the spiral butts up against the neighboring leg.

7 Repeat with the five remaining legs **(m)**.

TIP

After completing step 7, you can either hammer the outside edges of the spirals or leave the wire round. If the spirals were marred during shaping, hammering will flatten out any marks left by pliers. Lay the spirals on top of a bench block and hammer with the flat face of a chasing hammer.

8 Cut a 3-in. (89 mm) piece of 28-gauge (0.32 mm) wire. Hold a short tail in your non-dominant hand. Holding the tail wire in front, wrap around the upper leg, between the two legs and back around the lower leg **(n)**. This forms the beginning of a figure-8 pattern. Weave the wire back around the upper wire, completing the figure-8 **(o)**.

back of pendant

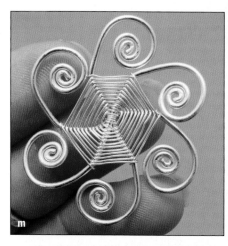

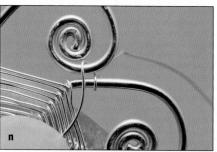

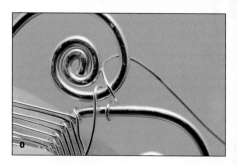

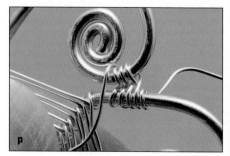

9 Repeat the same weave three more times, wrapping the upper and lower legs together with four figure-8 weaves **(p)**. To end the weave, wrap an extra time around one leg, trim and tuck down the end using chainnose pliers. Use chainnose pliers to squeeze the weaving together if it is too loose **(q)**. Weave together all of the legs.

10 Oxidize using liver of sulfur and polish using a polishing pad, steel wool or a polishing cloth. Open an 18-gauge (1.0 mm), 4.0 mm ID jump ring and slide it through one of the segments of the pendant and close the ring.

Wild heart necklace

A curvaceous borosilicate glass heart and etched metal circles nest into a copper squiggle. A handmade link chain and matching clasp complete a necklace with heavy-duty handmade appeal.

by Lisa Liddy

materials

- Copper wire, round, dead soft:
- 14 in. (30.5 cm) 12-gauge (2.1 mm)
- 5 ft. (1.5 m) 16-gauge (1.3 mm)
- 4 ft. (1 m) 24-gauge (0.5mm)
- 40 x 50 mm lampworked glass heart
- 2 ½-in. (13 mm) etched copper disks
- 2 ⅝-in. (16 mm) etched copper disks
- 2 10 mm copper jump rings
- Copper toggle

tools & supplies

- Wirework toolbox, p. 105
- Hole punch pliers
- Dapping block and punches

note

To make the focal wire element, use the provided template (Fig. 1) or draw an original squiggle template. If using an original template, start with 15–16 in. (38.1–40.6 cm) of wire to make certain there is enough to create the design. Although the template was provided by the designer, her necklaces vary slightly from the one provided.

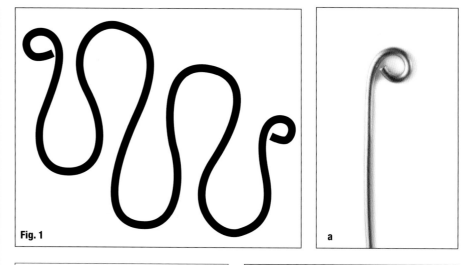

Fig. 1

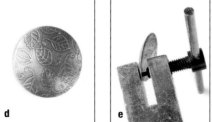

b

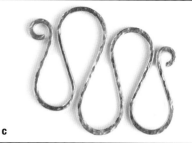

c

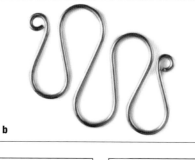

d

e

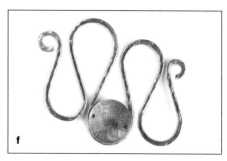

f

g

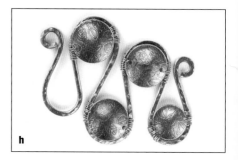

h

1 Using large roundnose pliers, make a loop on one flush-cut end of a 14-in. (35.6 cm) piece of 12-gauge (2.1 mm) wire **(a)**. Continue shaping to fit the template using your fingers and large wrap-and-tap or bail-making pliers. Trim off any extra wire, if needed. Finish the other end with a simple loop **(b)**.

2 When satisfied with the shape, use a bench block and chasing hammer to flatten and texture the wire **(c)**.

Attaching the etched disks

3 If your disks are already dapped, proceed to step 4. For flat etched disks, use a dapping block and punches to shape the circles into a cup shape **(d)**. Position the etching on the concave side of the dome.

4 Using a screw-down hole punch or hole-punch pliers, make two holes in the disk, 180 degrees from each other **(e)**. Position the punched disks on the focal wire to check their location, positioning the holes in the 3- and 9-o'clock positions. If needed, adjust the shape of the wire squiggle to fit the disks **(f)**.

5 Cut 6 in. (15.2 cm) of 24-gauge (0.5 mm) wire and attach one side of a domed disk to the focal wire with one or two wraps through the hole and around the squiggle. Continue wrapping around the squiggle five or six times on either side of the hole, and tuck the ends into the wrapping. Repeat on the other side of the disk **(g)**.

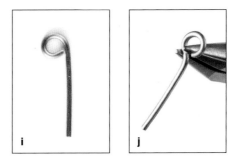

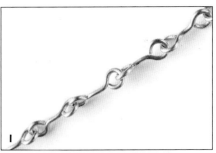

6 Repeat step 5 for the other domed disks, attaching them into the remaining loops in a design you find pleasing **(h)**. Leave an empty curve on the squiggle where the focal bead will be attached.

Make the chain

7 Measure and flush cut both ends of 48 pieces of 1¼-in. (32 mm) 16-gauge (1.3 mm) wire. Using roundnose pliers, make a simple round loop (Basics, p. 109), working where the plier jaws are ⅛ in. (3 mm) in diameter **(i)**. Using chainnose pliers, grasp the loop near the base and make a 90-degree bend in the wire **(j)**. Position the wire so you're looking through the loop and make a second simple loop on the other end of the wire. Using chainnose pliers, make a 90-degree bend at the base of the second loop. The loops will sit perpendicular to one another. Repeat for a total of 48 wire links. Set the links aside.

Assemble the necklace

8 Using two pairs of chainnose pliers, open a 10 mm jump ring and slide it through the hole in the focal bead and around a curve at the bottom of the squiggle. Close the jump ring **(k)**. The bead can be attached underneath a disk on one of the bottom squiggles if you opt to fill all the curves with disks.

9 Using chainnose pliers, open the loop on one link of chain and slide it to the bottom loop on the squiggle. Close the link. Repeat with another chain link on the other side of the squiggle. Continue adding links by opening one loop of one chain link, adding another chain link and closing the loop **(l)**.

10 Using two pairs of chainnose pliers, open the end links of the chain and slide an open 8 mm jump ring through the loop half of the toggle. Repeat to attach the other end of the chain to the clasp hook **(m)**. Adjust the length as needed by adding or removing links.

11 Add a patina and polish with a brass brush or fine steel wool to highlight the shapes and enhance the contrast of the finished necklace.

Custom bail and bead cages

Coil and spiral wire to make your own bail, spacers, and bead cages.

by Melody MacDuffee

materials

Necklace 20 in. (50.8 cm)
- Copper wire, round:
  - 16-gauge (1.29 mm), 6 ft. (1.8 m)
  - 22-gauge (0.64 mm), 18 in. (45.7 cm)
  - 24-gauge (0.51 mm), 6 yd. (5.5 m)
- 36 x 45 mm sea sediment jasper pendant, drilled front to back
- Krobo beads (www.soulofsomanya.net):
  - **4** 13 mm round beads, aqua
  - **12** 10–12 mm rondelles, translucent aqua
  - **12** 10–12 mm rondelles, translucent teal
  - **20** 10 mm flat spacers, caramel
  - **36** 7 mm cone beads, caramel
  - **12** 6 mm flat spacers, teal
  - **14** 6 mm flat spacers, caramel
- Flexible beading wire, 0.018
- **4** crimp beads, copper
- Hook-and-eye clasp, copper

tools & supplies
- Wirework toolbox, p. 105

Spacers

1 Cut 6 ft. (1.8 m) of 16-gauge (1.29 mm) wire. Using the wide end of your roundnose pliers, grasp the tip of the wire and turn the pliers to begin making a coil (Basics, p. 109), rotating so the wire's tip goes toward the tip of the pliers **(a)**. Continue until your coil has 54 wraps.

Using wire cutters, cut one wrap at a time to make each spacer. The spacers will have a bur from where they were cut. To remove the bur, either trim the wire with flush cutters or smooth it with a file.

Use two pairs of pliers to close each spacer, as you would close a jump ring (Basics, p. 110).

Bail

2 Using roundnose pliers, make a U bend at the center of the 16-gauge (1.29 mm) wire left over from step 1. Using a chasing hammer and bench block, hammer the U bend and ½ in. (13 mm) of wire on each side of it **(b)**.

3 At one end of the wire, make a coil, as in step 1, up to the flattened wire **(c)**.

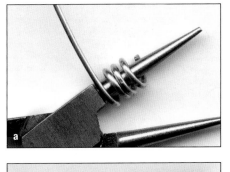
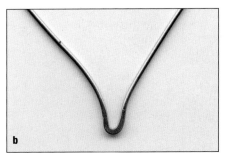

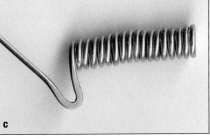
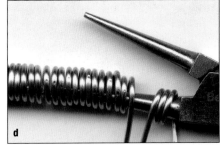

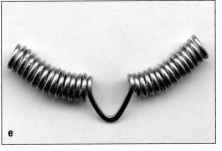
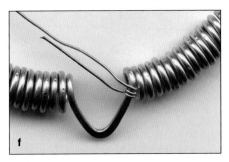

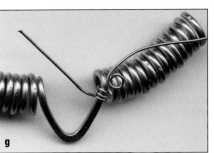
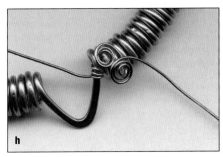

4 Flip the coil, and position it on the tip of the pliers so the U bend is near the wide end of the pliers. Starting after the flattened wire, make a coil out of the remaining straight wire. Make sure these wraps turn in the same direction as the wraps on the other coil **(d)**.

5 Count the wraps on both coils, and trim as needed to make them even. Use your fingers to slightly curve each side up **(e)**.

6 Cut 6 ft. (1.8 m) of 24-gauge (0.51 mm) wire. Leaving a 1-in. (25.5 mm) tail, wrap the wire three times around the bail wire where one coil begins **(f)**.

7 Using roundnose pliers, make a small loop **(g)**. Using chainnose pliers, grasp across the loop and make a spiral (Basics, p. 109). Make a loop in the opposite direction, then make that loop into another spiral **(h)**. Continue making loops and spirals **(i)**, changing direction

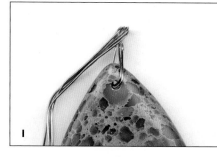

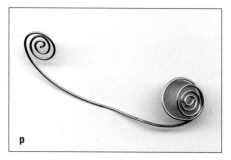

as necessary to create a dense lace that covers the coil. To periodically anchor the lace, bring the wire in between the coil's wraps as needed.

8 When the coil is covered, make several wraps around and/or into the coil to anchor the wire. Trim the tails **(j)**.

9 Repeat steps 6–8 on the other coil **(k)**.

Pendant

10 Cut two 1-yd. (91.4 cm) pieces of 24-gauge (0.51 mm) wire. Align the wires to use them as one, and center a pendant on both wires. Bring the wire ends together above the pendant and, using all four ends as one piece of wire, make the first half of a wrapped loop (Basics, p. 110) **(l)**. Slide the bail's U bend into the loop **(m)**, and complete the wraps, but don't trim the wires. Continue wrapping the wires around the top of the pendant as far down as desired **(n)**. Trim the wires at the back of the pendant, and hide the tails under the wraps **(o)**.

Bead cages

11 Cut 9 in. (22.9 cm) of 22-gauge (0.64 mm) wire. At each end of the wire, make a 10 mm (⅜-in.) spiral, leaving about 5 in. (12.7 cm) between the spirals. Position a spiral over one end of a 13 mm round aqua bead **(p)**. Wrap the wire around the bead until you can nudge the second spiral to cap the other end of the bead **(q)**. Repeat with another 13 mm bead.

Assembly

On 22 in. (55.9 cm) of beading wire, center two 7 mm cone beads. Nestle the cone beads into the bail's U bend, and guide each wire end through a coil of the bail.

On each end, string beads as desired or as follows: an aqua rondelle, a teal rondelle, an aqua rondelle, three spacers, three cone beads, three spacers, a 6 mm caramel spacer, a caged bead, a 6 mm caramel spacer, three spacers, three cone beads, three spacers, an aqua rondelle, a teal rondelle, an aqua rondelle, three spacers, a cone bead, a 6 mm teal spacer, a 6 mm caramel spacer, three 10 mm caramel spacers, a 6 mm caramel spacer, a 6 mm teal spacer, a cone bead, three spacers, a 13 mm round aqua bead, three spacers, three cone beads, a 6 mm teal spacer, three spacers, a 6 mm caramel spacer, an aqua rondelle, a teal rondelle, an aqua rondelle, a 6 mm caramel spacer, three spacers, a 6 mm teal spacer, three cone beads, a 6 mm teal spacer, a 6 mm caramel spacer, a 6 mm teal spacer, and three cone beads.

On one end, string a crimp bead and half of a clasp. Go back through the crimp bead, crimp the crimp bead by squeezing it shut with crimping pliers, and trim the tail. Repeat at the other end.

Sea turtle pendant

Frame an ocean-colored disk-shaped bead with shining silver wire to create a friendly little sea dweller.

by Tracey Knaus

materials

Pendant 2½ in. (64 mm)

- Silver wire, round:
  - 24 in. (61 cm) 20-gauge (0.8 mm)
  - 52 in. (1.3 m) 26-gauge (0.4 mm)
- **1** 1¼-in. (32 mm) disk-shaped bead
- **1** 8 mm round bead
- **10–15** 11º seed beads

tools & supplies

- Flatnose pliers
- Roundnose pliers
- Wire cutters
- Steel bench block or anvil
- Hammer (chasing, goldsmith's, or light utility)

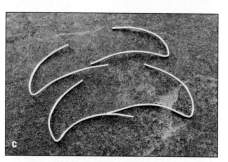

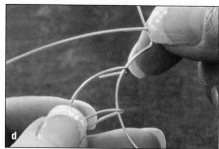

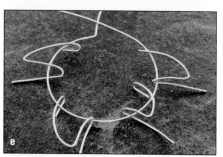

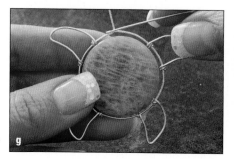

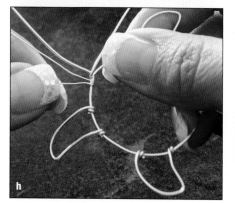

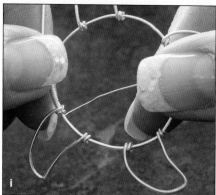

keep them loosely attached to the frame **(e)**.

4 Place a flipper where you'd like it to be on the frame, and wrap the tail of each hook one or two times around the frame to secure the flipper. Trim and tuck the wire ends (Basics, p. 109). Repeat to position and secure the other three flippers **(f)**. (You'll still be able to move the flippers later if you want to reposition them, but they won't slide loosely.)

5 Set the disk bead in the frame. Reshape the frame if necessary, make a U-bend in the straight tail of the frame wire, and hook it around the wire you bent in step 1 **(g)**. This will hold the body of the turtle in shape.

6 Cut 52 in. (1.3 m) of 26-gauge (wrapping) wire. Beginning at the "head," coil the wrapping wire around the frame (Basics, p. 109) leaving a 3-in.

1 Cut a 12-in. (30.5 cm) piece of 20-gauge (frame) wire. Shape the frame wire around a 1¼-in. (32 mm) disk-shaped bead **(a)**, leaving a tail of wire at each end. Make a 90-degree upward bend in one of the tail wires; this is where the turtle's "head" will be on the finished piece.

2 Cut four 3-in. (76 mm) pieces of 20-gauge (flipper) wire. Using flatnose pliers, make a roughly 90-degree bend at the centerpoint of each flipper wire **(b)**. Then use your fingers to bend and shape the wires to look like flippers **(c)**.

3 Place each flipper against the frame, and determine how far you want the flipper to extend. Make a U-bend in each wire end to hook around the frame **(d)**. When you are done, you will have four flippers with bent ends that will

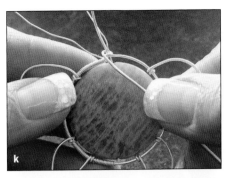

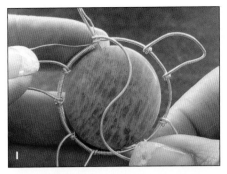

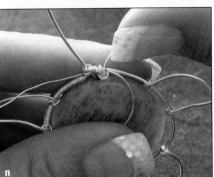

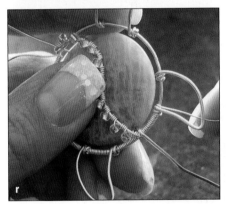

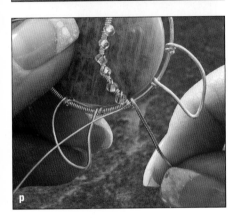

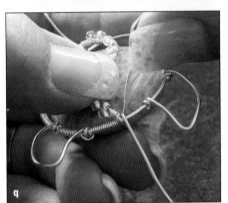

(76 mm) tail **(h)**. Continue coiling until you reach the first flipper. (If you need to reposition the flipper, now's the time!) Wrap around the place where the flipper meets the frame to secure it **(i)**. Continue coiling around the frame until you reach the bottom of the frame, opposite the head.

7 Set the disk bead in the frame. Feed the wrapping wire at the bottom of the frame through the hole of the bead so that it extends at the top of the frame **(j)**.

8 Lay the wrapping wire alongside the frame wire's vertical tail. Wrap the second frame wire tail once around both wires **(k)**, and then bring it down to the bottom of the frame, forming it into a curved "yin/yang" shape **(l)**.

9 Once you have the desired shape, coil the wrapping wire around both the frame and the curved wire four times **(m)**. String a seed bead onto the wrapping wire **(n)**, and make four wraps around just the curved wire. Continue adding beads to the curved wire, with four complete wraps between beads, until you reach the bottom of the frame **(o)**.

10 Wrap the tail of the curved wire once around the bottom of the frame **(p)**. Then, use the wrapping wire to make one wrap around the curved and frame wires **(q)**.

11 Continue coiling around the frame as in step 6 **(r)**.

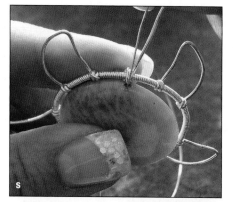

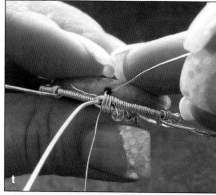

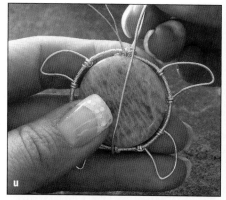

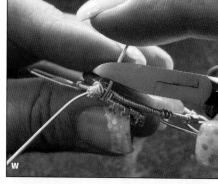

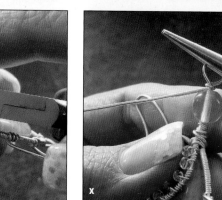

12 Once you reach the top of the frame, feed the wrapping wire through the disk bead, bringing it back to the bottom of the frame **(s)**. Wrap around the bottom of the curved wire **(t)**, and feed the wrapping wire back up through the disk bead to the top of the frame again. Do this three times. This ensures that the relatively heavy bead won't break the smaller-gauge wire, and also gives the bead added security in the frame.

13 Bring the tail of the curved wire up behind the disk bead to the top of the frame **(u)**. With both tails of the wrapping wire, make several wraps around the frame wire tail **(v)** and the tail of the curved wire. Trim and tuck the wrapping wire and the tail of the curved wire **(w)**.

14 String an 8 mm bead onto the frame wire tail. Using roundnose pliers, make a loop above the bead. Wrap once above the bead **(x)**, bring the wire across the front of the bead **(y)**, and wrap two or three times below the bead. Trim and tuck the wire.

15 On a bench block, lightly hammer the tips of the flippers **(z)**; this work-hardens them and gives them a bit more stability. String the pendant as desired.

RainChain necklace

Create a stunning necklace with steel wire using the Now That's a Jig! tool and a downloadable template.

by Brenda Schweder

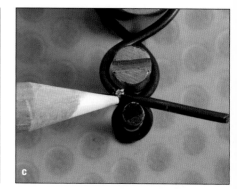

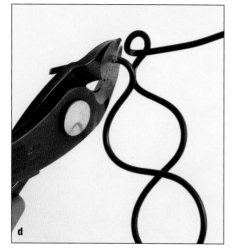

Jig setup

1 Download the RainChain template for the Now That's a Jig! (NTaJ!) at www.now-thats-a-jig.com, and print it onto vellum paper. Place the pattern on the jig bed, aligning the corner holes. Punch through the corner holes with the PatternPunchr, and insert CornerTaks.

2 Use the PatternPunchr to punch holes for the appropriate pegs on the pattern, and screw them in. Punch holes for the SwiveLok as indicated on the pattern, and partially screw it in **(a)**.

Focal components

3 Flush-cut one 12-in. (30.5 cm), two 10-in. (25.4 cm), and two 8-in. (20.3 cm) pieces of 16-gauge wire.

4 Center the 12-in. (30.5 cm) piece of wire between the 1-in. (25.5 mm) round peg and SwiveLok. Turn the SwiveLok counterclockwise to trap the wire, and then tighten the screw.

5 Wrap the wire around the pegs, crisscrossing between each peg pair. End by wrapping one side around the

bottom-most peg and overlapping between the two smallest pegs **(b)**.

6 Use a white charcoal pencil to mark each end of the wire just before it meets the intersecting wire above or below it **(c)**.

7 Loosen the SwiveLok, and turn it away from the trapped wire and peg. Lift the component off the pegs with the WireLiftr. Flush-cut the wire ends at the marks made in step 6 **(d)**.

8 Place the component on a bench block or anvil. Use a utility or ball-peen hammer to work-harden and texture the component, being careful not to strike where the wire overlaps **(e)**.

TIP

Hammering will slightly distort the shape and openings. Fit the component back on the jig to adjust.

9 Repeat steps 4–8 for the 10-in. (25.4 cm) pieces of wire using the four smallest pegs, and repeat again for the 8-in. (20.3 cm) pieces of wire using the three smallest pegs.

10 Clean each component with steel wool. To seal, apply Renaissance wax sparingly, and buff with a soft cloth.

Chain links

11 Flush-cut a 24-in. (61 cm) piece of 16-gauge wire. Leaving a 2-in. (51 mm) tail to use as a lever, wrap the wire tightly around the DoubleDekr ½-in. (13 mm) peg to make a coil of 12 complete rings. Use the WireLiftr to compress the wire on the peg as you wind **(f)**.

12 Remove the coil from the peg. Use a jeweler's saw to cut 12 chain links as you would to cut jump rings (Basics, p. 110). Use a needle file to remove any burrs.

13 Hammer, clean, and seal the chain links as before.

Staples

14 Flush-cut a 35-in. (88.9 cm) piece of 18-gauge wire, and hammer, clean, and seal it as before. Flush-cut the wire into 16 2-in. (51 mm) pieces and one 3-in. (76 mm) piece. Set the 3-in. (76 mm) piece aside for step 19.

materials

Necklace 18 in. (45.7 cm)

- Dark annealed steel wire:
  - 6 ft. (1.8 m) 16-gauge (1.6 mm)
  - 35 in. (88.9 cm) 18-gauge (1.2 mm)
  - 50 in. (1.2 m) 28-gauge (0.4 mm)
- **1** 27 mm round crystal stone (Swarovski #1201, crystal with foil)
- **1** 16 mm crystal button (Swarovski #3015, crystal)
- **1** 10 mm two-hole sew-on faceted flat-back stone (Swarovski, crystal)
- **1** 4 mm bicone crystal (Swarovski, crystal)

tools & supplies

- **2** pairs of chainnose, flatnose, and/or bentnose pliers
- Nylon-jaw pliers
- Flush cutters strong enough to cut 16-gauge (1.3 mm) steel wire
- Now That's a Jig! Starter Kit (www.riogrande.com)
- Now That's a Jig! accessories (www.now-thats-a-jig.com):
  - SwiveLok
  - WireLiftr
  - BigRound peg mix (1 in., 1½ in., 1¾ in.)
  - RainChain downloadable template
  - PatternPunchr and CornerTaks
  - DoubleDekr screw
- Vellum paper
- White charcoal pencil
- Steel bench block or anvil
- 4–6 oz. utility or ball-peen hammer
- Steel wool (fine, #00) or wire brush
- Renaissance wax and soft cloth
- Jeweler's saw with 2/0 blade
- Needle file
- 2 x 2-in. (51 x 51 mm) tissue square

15 Center a 2-in. (51 mm) piece between the staple peg setup and SwiveLok. Turn the SwiveLok to trap the wire, and tighten the screw. Wrap the ends of the wire down and around the ⅛-in. (3 mm) pegs **(g)**.

16 Loosen and remove the SwiveLok, and bring the wire ends back up between the two pegs. With the white pencil, mark the cut lines **(h)**.

17 Lift the staple off the jig bed, and flush-cut the ends at the marks **(i)**.

18 Repeat steps 15–17 to make a total of 16 staples.

TIP

An 18-in. (45.7 cm) necklace will have six link/staple combinations on each side. The remaining four staples are used to connect the focal components. Each additional link/staple combination lengthens each side of the necklace by 1 in. (25.5 mm).

Hook clasp

19 Trap the 3-in. (76 mm) wire between the hook-clasp peg setup and the SwiveLok, and tighten the screw.

20 Tightly wrap the right side of the wire counterclockwise around the ⅛-in. (3 mm) right-most peg. Wrap the left side of the wire counterclockwise around the ⅛-in. (3 mm) left-most peg, bringing it up and over the tip of the triangular peg **(j)**.

21 Use chainnose pliers to pinch the wire at the tip of the triangular peg to make a sharp angle.

22 Mark the cut lines, and loosen the SwiveLok. Lift the hook off the jig bed, and trim the excess wire. Forge the tip of the hook by hammering it, and file if necessary to remove any burrs.

Necklace assembly

23 Open a chain link the same way you would open a jump ring (Basics, p. 110). Insert a chain link into a staple, and close the link. Continue attaching chain links and staples for a total of six links, beginning and ending with a link, and making sure the staples all face the same way. This chain will form one side of the necklace. Repeat to make the chain for the other side of the necklace.

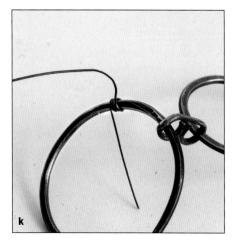

k

l

m

TIP

Since the loops are on the back side of the staples, attach the chain links and focal components with their back sides facing up so they will face the correct way when worn.

24 Arrange the focal components from smallest to largest to smallest, and place a chain on each side of this arrangement. Open the staple loops as if they were jump rings, and attach the focal components to one another and to the chains.

25 Open a chain link on one end of the necklace, insert the small loop of the hook clasp, and close the link.

Crystal embellishments

26 Cut, clean, and seal 50 in. (1.2 m) of 28-gauge wire. Cut one 1-yd. (91.4 cm) (long) piece of wire, two 6-in. (15.2 cm) (medium) pieces of wire, and one 2-in. (51 mm) (short) piece of wire.

27 Hold the long wire against the largest circle of the center focal component so that a 1-in. (25.5 mm) tail exits the center of the circle on the front of the component. Make two or three tight wraps around the circle, ending with the wire coming up on the outside of the component **(k)**.

28 Wrap the 27 mm round crystal stone in a 2 x 2-in. (51 x 51 mm) tissue square, and place it in the large circle. Pull the wire over the tissue-covered stone, and make one or two wraps around the opposite edge of the circle **(l)**. Pull the wire across the back of the stone, and make one or two wraps.

n

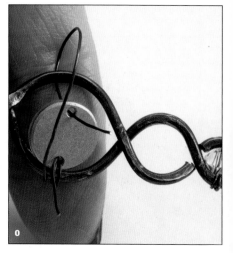

o

29 Make six to eight more sets of wraps, each time pulling the wire across the stone in a free-form manner. Leave room for the staples at the 10 and 2 o'clock positions. Trim and tuck the wire ends (Basics, p. 109), and tear away the tissue.

TIP

Use nylon-jaw pliers to straighten the wire as you wrap, especially the wire that crosses the face of the stone.

30 Thread a medium piece of wire through the 16 mm crystal button, leaving one end of the wire slightly longer than the other. Thread the longer end of the wire through the button again **(m)**.

31 Place the button in the second-largest circle of the center focal component. With each end of the wire, make two to three wraps around the circle at the 9 and 3 o'clock positions **(n)**. Thread the ends of the wire back through the button, and trim.

32 Place the remaining medium piece of wire across the back of the 10 mm sew-on stone. Place the stone face up in the third-largest circle of the center focal component. Bring the ends of the wire over the circle at the 9 and 3 o'clock positions, and go down through the side holes of the stone **(o)**. Repeat two to three times, and trim and tuck the wire ends.

33 Thread the short piece of wire through the 4 mm bicone crystal, and place the bicone in the smallest circle of the center focal component. With each end of the wire, make two wraps around the circle at the 9 and 3 o'clock positions. Trim and tuck the wire ends.

Squarely crystallized pendant

A square crystal takes center stage in this wire-wrapped pendant embellished with spirals and bicone crystals.

by Lisa Niven Kelly

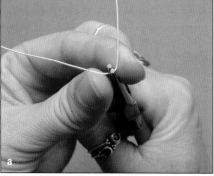

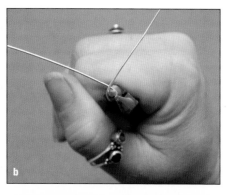

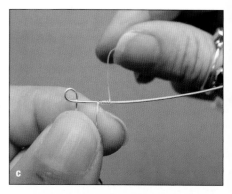

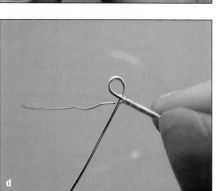

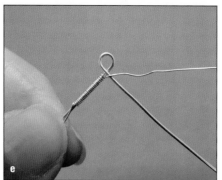

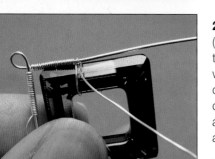

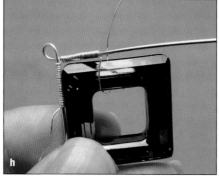

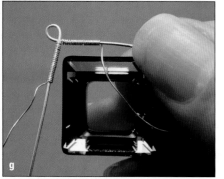

1 Cut a 5-in. (12.7 cm) piece of 22-gauge (frame) wire. Position the center of the wire on the roundnose pliers 2–3 mm from the tip. Bend the ends of the wire up toward each other **(a)**, making sure that the ends are the same length. Continue bending the ends past each other until they form a right angle **(b)**.

2 Cut 1 yd. (91.4 cm) of 28-gauge (wrapping) wire, and make a bend in the wire at the center. Hold the frame wire as shown in **(c)**, and place the bend of the wrapping wire on the right leg of the frame wire near the loop. Coil around the frame wire (Basics, p. 109) away from the loop for ⁵⁄₁₆ in. (6 mm) **(d)**.

TIP
Sometimes the start of a coil isn't as tight as it could be. If needed, undo the first few wraps to clean up that end, but make sure you add a few wraps to the other end of the coil to keep the length at ⁵⁄₁₆ in. (6 mm).

3 Slide the coil against the loop of the frame wire, and bring the tail end of the wrapping wire around the back of the

loop **(e)**. Continue to coil around the other leg of the frame wire for ⁵⁄₁₆ in. (6 mm).

TIP
Because I like to build a coil to the right using my right hand as my coiling hand, I flip the frame to begin coiling around the other leg **(e)**.

4 Position one corner of a 20 mm square crystal pendant at a slight distance from the corner of the coiled frame wire **(f)**.

5 Bring the wrapping wire between the frame wire and the square **(g)**, and continue through the center of the square going from front to back. Bend the wire up behind the square, and pull tight **(h)**.

materials

Green necklace 17 in. (43.2 cm)

- 18 in. (45.7 cm) 22-gauge (0.6 mm) sterling silver wire, round, dead soft or half hard
- 6½ ft. (2.0 m) 28-gauge (0.32 mm) sterling silver wire, round, dead soft
- **1** 20 mm square crystal pendant (Swarovski, Bermuda blue)
- **5** 4 mm bicone crystals (Swarovski, light sapphire)
- **8** 3 mm bicone crystals (Swarovski, Montana blue and erinite)
- **5** 2-in. (51 mm) 24-gauge (0.5 mm) sterling silver ball head pins
- **6** 18-gauge (1.0 mm), 4 mm inner diameter (ID) sterling silver jump rings
- 16 in. (40.6 cm) chain
- Lobster claw clasp

tools & supplies

- **2** pairs of chainnose, flatnose, and/or bentnose pliers
- Roundnose pliers
- Wire cutters
- Steel bench block or anvil
- Rawhide or plastic mallet

Crystal colors for purple necklace

- 20 mm square crystal pendant (Swarovski, volcano)
- 4 mm bicone crystals (Swarovski, purple and lime AB)
- 3 mm bicone crystals (Swarovski, fuchsia and purple velvet)

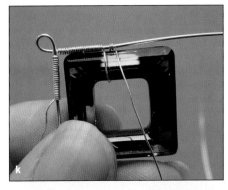

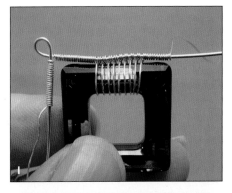

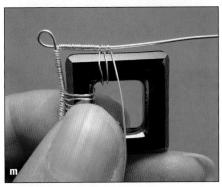

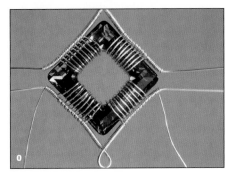

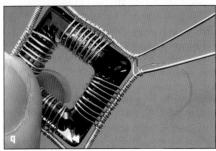

6 Bring the wrapping wire between the frame wire and square again **(i)**. Make one tight wrap around the frame wire **(j)**. Make one more tight wrap around the frame wire **(k)**.

7 Repeat steps 5 and 6 to make a total of nine single wraps through the square and nine pairs of wraps around the frame wire.

TIP

The wrapping wire will always be forming a figure 8 around the frame wire and the square. It must always go between the frame wire and square before transitioning to the next wrap. You never want the wrapping wire go straight from the frame wire over the side of the square.

8 Coil around the frame wire for the remainder of the length of the square **(l)**. Trim and tuck this end of the wrapping wire (Basics, p. 109).

9 With the other end of the wrapping wire, repeat steps 5–8 for the other leg of the frame wire.

TIP

If you like to work from left to right, flip the frame over so the back of the crystal is facing you **(m)**.

10 With the tip of your chainnose pliers, bend the frame wire up at a slight angle so that it's parallel with the mitered facet at the corner of the square **(n)**. Repeat for the other end of the frame wire.

11 Repeat steps 1–10 to add a second frame wire, but use 3½ ft. (1.1 m) of wrapping wire in step 2, and don't trim the wrapping wire in step 8 **(o)**.

12 Bring one end of the wrapping wire up between the two frame wires, and make two wraps around the top frame wire **(p)**. Bring the wrapping wire down between the two frame wires, and make two wraps around the bottom frame wire **(q)**.

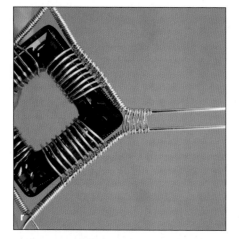

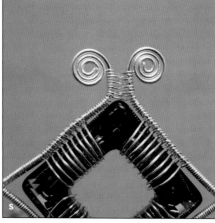

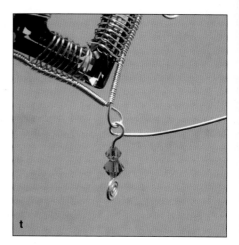

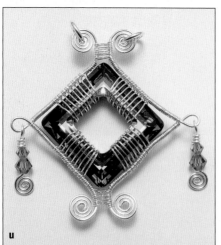

note

If you like antiqued wire, you can patinate the finished piece with liver of sulfur (Basics, p. 110). If you are concerned about liver of sulfur affecting your crystal, you can pre-patinate your wire, head pins, and jump rings. Work with the metal darkened, and then polish when finished. Do not put the pendant in a tumbler for a high-polish finish. The tumbler will ruin the back coating on the crystal.

13 Repeat step 12 to weave ⅛ in. (3 mm) **(r)**. Trim and tuck this end of the wrapping wire.

14 Trim the frame wires on this end so they are the same length. Form a spiral (Basics, p. 109) with one frame wire, leaving a hole in the center of the spiral large enough for an 18-gauge jump ring. Repeat to form a spiral on the other frame wire **(s)**. Rest the spirals on a bench block, and use a rawhide or plastic mallet to lightly tap the spirals to work-harden them.

15 Repeat steps 12–14 for the other ends of the frame wires.

16 Cut a 4-in. (10.2 cm) piece of 22-gauge wire. Form a spiral on one end to make a spiral head pin. String a 4 mm bicone crystal and a 3 mm bicone crystal, and make the first half of a wrapped loop (Basics, p. 109). Attach the loop to the frame wire loop on one side of the pendant **(t)**, and complete the wraps. Repeat this step to make and attach a bicone dangle to the frame wire loop on the other side of the pendant.

17 Open a 4 mm jump ring (Basics, p. 110), slide it through one spiral at the top of the pendant, and close the jump ring. Repeat to attach a jump ring to the other spiral at the top of the pendant **(u)**.

18 Using ball head pins, make five bicone dangles as shown in **(v)**, noting that two pairs of dangles are connected by their loops.

19 Attach two 4 mm jump rings to the bottom spirals as in step 17. Open another 4 mm jump ring, and add the crystal dangles in the order shown in **(v)**. Slide the jump ring through the two bottom jump rings, and close the jump ring.

20 Open a jump ring at the top of the pendant, attach an 8-in. (20.3 cm) piece of chain, and close the jump ring. Repeat to attach another 8-in. (20.3 cm) chain to the other jump ring.

21 Use a 4 mm jump ring to attach a lobster claw clasp to the end of one of the chains.

Freeform woven swirls pendant

Woven swirls transform a simple border wrap into a pendant full of curvaceous whimsy. Layered wires and an asymmetrical design create a complex look built using basic wire techniques. Make spirals, turn round loops, coil and weave for detailed results.

by Donna Spadafore

materials

Pendant 51 x 32 mm (2 x 1¼ in.)

- Copper, brass, or sterling silver wire:
  - 52 in. (1.3 meters), 20-gauge square, half-hard wire
  - 8 in (20.3 cm), 20-gauge half-round, half-hard wire
  - 22 ft. (5.8 meters), 28-gauge (0.32 mm) round, dead-soft wire
  - 12.7 cm (5 in.), 26-gauge (0.40 mm) round, dead-soft wire
- 25 mm (1-in.) round cabochon
- 4 mm round bead

tools & supplies

- Wirework toolbox, p. 105
- 8 mm mandrel or bail-making pliers

1 Cut four 13-in. (33 cm) pieces of 20-gauge (0.8 mm) square, half-hard wire. Place a mark at the center of all four wires. Measure and mark 10 mm (⅜ in.) to the left and right of the center. Using a 2½-in. (64 mm) piece of 20-gauge (0.8 mm), half-round wire, wrap the wires together at the left- and right-of-center marks five times. Trim close to the wrapped wires **(a)**.

2 Shape the wrapped wires around the cabochon. Position the center mark at the center of the bottom of the cab **(b)**.

3 Mark the wires where they overlap at the top of the cabochon. Hold the wires around the stone and check the fit **(c)**. Make small adjustments until the wire fits around the cabochon. Bend the wires up to about a 90-degree angle **(d)**.

TIP

A wire wrap to trap a cabochon is termed a border wrap. Usually in a border wrap, the wires are snug against the stone. For this project, a small amount of space makes it easier to attach the swirls to the frame.

4 Use a 4-in. (10.2 cm) piece of 20-gauge (0.8 mm), half-round wire to wrap the wires together seven times at the top of the frame **(e)**.

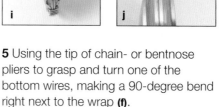

5 Using the tip of chain- or bentnose pliers to grasp and turn one of the bottom wires, making a 90-degree bend right next to the wrap **(f)**.

6 Repeat step 5 on each side of the bundles and on both wires at the top of the frame, creating a basket **(g)**.

7 Put the cabochon face down into the basket. Repeat steps 5 and 6, to shape a basket on the back of the cabochon that matches the one on the front **(h)**.

8 Separate two wires from the back of the bundle at the top of the frame and bend them slightly backward **(i)**.

9 Cut a 3-ft. (91.4 cm) piece of 28-gauge (0.32 mm) wire and wrap it around one of the back wires four or five times just above the bundle. Cut the starting tail wire and press it against the frame wire **(j)**.

10 Use the 28-gauge (0.32 mm) wire to bind together the two wires in a figure-8 pattern. Weave a 40 mm (1⁹⁄₁₆-in.) long section. Wrap the end of the 28-gauge (0.32 mm) wire around one of the

frame wires five times **(k)**. Flush cut the wrapping wire close to the frame wire. Tuck the end against the frame with chainnose pliers.

TIP

For the remainder of this project, all 28-gauge (0.32 mm) wires will be secured as shown in step 10.

11 Measure 9.5 mm (⅜ in.) past the end of the woven section and trim the wire ends. Shape the woven section over the 8 mm mandrel so that the end of the woven wires rests just above the bottom basket wire **(l)**.

12 Use roundnose pliers to loop the ends of the wires underneath the bottom basket wire. Use chainnose pliers to close the loops. Use your fingers to press the woven section against the

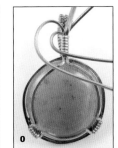

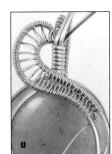

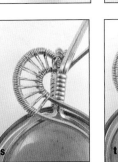

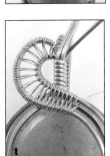

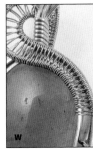

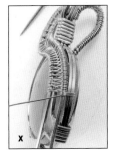

back of the cabochon, creating a tear-drop-shaped bail at the top **(m)**.

13 Turn the pendant over and separate the remaining wires into three sections. The two front center wires are one section. The two back wires on the left are another section. The two wires on the right form the third section **(n)**.

14 Shape the two left wires into a curve starting from the side of the bail. For this pendant, the wires are about 4–5 mm apart where they meet the left side of the curve **(o)**. The measurement does not have to be exact but is provided as a guideline.

TIP

For the remainder of this project, all 28-gauge (0.32 mm) wires will be attached as in step 15.

15 Cut a 5-ft. (1.5 m) piece of 28-gauge (0.32 mm) wire. Attach it to the upper curve wire by wrapping it around the frame wire five times. Cut the beginning wire tail and press it against the frame wire using chainnose pliers **(p)**.

16 Pass the 28-gauge (0.32 mm) wire between the two frame wires and wrap it one full time around the lower wire **(q)**.

17 Pass the wire back between the two frame wires and make multiple wraps around the upper wire **(r)**.

TIP

While weaving around the curve, the number of wraps around the outer frame wire will vary. Imagine that you are cutting a cake from one edge to the center. When you pull the wire across the two frame wires and the angle looks perfect for cutting that slice of cake, then you have wrapped enough times on the outer wire (18). Wrap all the way around once and then cross back to the outer wire.

18 Continue weaving around the curve until approximately ⅛ in. (3 mm) before the frame wires cross over the center bail. Curve the wires to mimic the shape of the basket wires on the opposite side of the bail **(s)**.

19 Keep weaving, wrapping completely around each frame wire before crossing between the wires, until the wire curves back toward the center. At that point, start wrapping two full times around the outer wire and one full wrap around the inner wire **(t)**.

20 Keep weaving just a little bit further around the curve. Viewing the pendant as a clock face, stop weaving at approximately the 2 o'clock position **(u)**. Secure the weaving to the pendant by wrapping the wire once around the inner frame wire and the basket wire **(v)**.

21 Continue weaving until reaching the 3 o'clock position **(w)**. Secure the outer frame wire to the cabochon frame wires by wrapping the outer frame wire twice to the double wires on the side of the cabochon basket **(x)**.

22 Use roundnose pliers and fingers to shape the two frame wires into another swirl, sweeping across the cabochon toward the top of the pendant **(y)**.

23 Continue the figure 8-weave around this swirl, changing the number of wraps on the outer wire to divide the space into wedges. Adjust the size and shape of the frame wires, forming the inner wire into a small loop **(z)**.

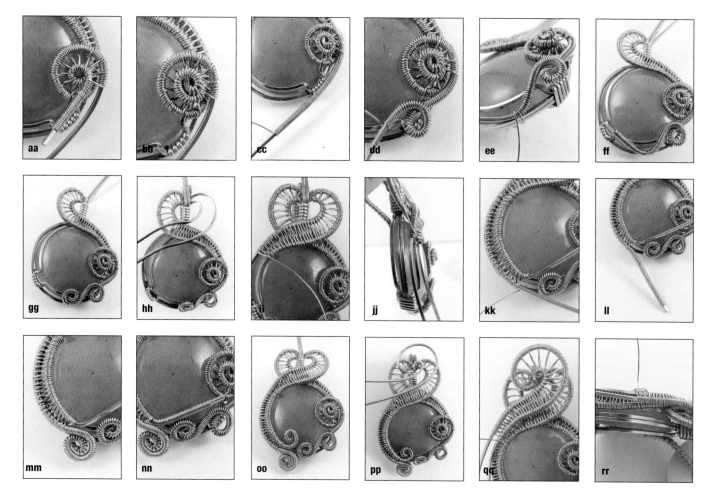

24 Coil a ½-in. (13 mm) section around the inside frame wire. Cut the frame wire ⅛ in. (3 mm) past the end of the coil **(aa)**.

25 Use roundnose pliers to shape a loop from the bare frame wire, starting a spiral. Use chainnose pliers to form a spiral from the coil-wrapped frame wire (Basics, p. 109). Press the coiled spiral into the center of the swirl **(bb)**.

26 Cut a 2-ft. (61 cm) length of 28-gauge (0.32 mm) wire and attach it to the second frame wire as described in step 15. Coil a 1¾-in. (44 mm) section around the frame wire **(cc)**.

27 Shape the coiled frame wire into a loop, bringing the end back toward the bottom of the pendant as it comes out of the loop **(dd)**.

28 Continue coiling onto the frame wire until the coil sits next to the cabochon frame. Wrap twice around the frame wire and side wires of the cabochon basket **(ee)**.

29 Coil a ½-in. (13 mm) section beyond the anchor point on the side. Cut the frame wire ⅛ in. (3 mm) past the end of the coil **(ff)**.

30 Use roundnose pliers to shape a loop from the bare frame wire, starting a spiral. Use chainnose pliers to spiral the coil-encased end of the wire toward the anchor point. Position the spiral near the center of the pendant **(gg)**.

31 Shape the two right hand wires to create a mirror image of the other side, creating a heart shape **(hh)**.

32 Working with a 5-ft. (1.5 m) piece of 28-gauge (0.32 mm) wire, attach and weave the right side in the same manner as the left side. Stop weaving at the 10 o'clock position **(ii)**.

33 Attach the inner wire to the cabochon basket wire by wrapping them together **(jj)**.

34 Continue weaving in the same manner all the way to the bottom of the pendant. Use two wraps to attach the inner frame wire to the cabochon basket **(kk)**.

35 Bring the weaving wire back to the outer frame wire and coil a ¾-in. (19 mm) section. Cut the frame wire ⅛ in. (3 mm) past the end of the coil **(ll)**.

36 Use roundnose pliers to shape a loop from the bare frame wire, starting a spiral. Use chainnose pliers to finish forming the coil-encased frame wire into a spiral, turning the initial loop toward the outside of the frame **(mm)**.

37 Attach a 8-in. (20.3 cm) piece of 28-gauge (0.32 mm) wire to the inner wire and coil a ½-in. (13 mm) section. Cut the frame wire ⅛ in. (3 mm) past the end of the coil **(nn)**.

38 Use roundnose pliers to shape a loop from the bare frame wire, starting a spiral. Use chainnose pliers to finish

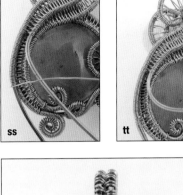

forming a spiral from the coil-encased frame wire, turning the initial loop toward the top of the pendant. Press the spiral as close as possible to the face of the cabochon (oo).

39 Sweep the remaining straight right-hand frame wire into a loop about ⅛ in. (3 mm) in diameter. Shape the other wire into a sweeping curve to create a ¾-in. (19 mm) diameter circle (pp).

40 Attach a 5-ft. (1.5 m) piece of 28-gauge (0.32 mm) wire. Weave around the curve and down the top of the side of the pendant as in steps 15–20. Stop weaving at the 10 o'clock position (qq).

41 Wrap the outer wire from this swirl to the outer wire of the previous swirl (rr).

TIP

If you have difficulty passing the 28-gauge (0.32 mm) wire through the weave to attach the swirls together, use a straight pin to create a small gap where the wire can fit through.

42 Coil around to the 9 o'clock position. Attach the wire to the outer wire of the previous swirl as in step 41 (ss).

43 Coil a ¾-in. (19 mm) section past the anchor point. Cut the frame wire ⅛ in. (3 mm) past the end of the coil (tt).

44 Attach an 8-in. (20.3 cm) piece of 28-gauge (0.32 mm) wire to the inner wire and coil a ½-in. (13 mm) section. Cut the frame wire ⅛ in. (3 mm) past the end of the coil (uu).

45 On both wire ends, use roundnose pliers to shape a loop from the bare frame wire, starting to roll the spiral upward, toward the top of the pendant. Use chainnose pliers to finish forming spirals from both coil-encased frame wires. Press the spirals into place (vv).

46 Cut a 5-in. (12.7 cm) piece of 26-gauge (0.4 mm) wire. Center a 4 mm bead on the wire and bend the wire 90 degrees on each side of the bead (ww). Position the bead in the center of the third swirl at the top of the pendant. Push the wire through the weave in the front swirl and both of the rear swirls near the top of the curves (xx).

47 Wrap the 26-gauge (0.4 mm) wire four times around the outer wires at the top of the two rear swirls. Flush cut the ends and tuck the wire against the frame using chainnose pliers (yy).

TIP

This project can easily be adapted to cabochons of different sizes and shapes. The swirl patterns in this lesson are more of a suggestion. You can alter them to fit any stone using the same techniques shown here.

EARRINGS
&
RINGS

Waterfall fern earrings

Follow a template to make earrings with graceful swirls.

by Erin Paton

materials

Earrings

- Sterling silver wire:
  - 18-gauge (1.02 mm), round, dead-soft, 11 in. (27.9 cm)
  - 20-gauge (0.81 mm), round, half-hard, 5½ in. (14 cm)
  - 22-gauge (0.64 mm) square, 11 in. (27.9 cm)
  - 28-gauge (0.32 mm), round, dead-soft, 4 ft. 4 in. (1.4 m)
- Seamless spacer beads:
  - 2 4 mm
  - 2 3 mm
  - 34 2 mm

tools & supplies

- Wirework toolbox, p. 105
- Ring mandrel (U.S. sizes)

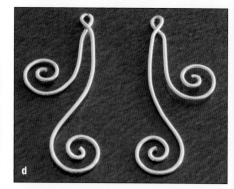

Earring frames

1 Cut 5½ in. (14 cm) of 18-gauge (1.02 mm) wire, and make a mark 2⅜ in. (60 mm) from one end. Using roundnose pliers, grasp the wire at the mark, and cross the longer wire end over the shorter wire end, making a loop **(a)**.

2 Using roundnose pliers, grasp the end of the shorter wire, and make an open spiral (Basics, p. 109) **(b)**. Leave the end loop of the spiral open so you can later fit a loop of twisted wire into it.

Template

3 Below the top loop, use roundnose pliers to grasp each wire end, and bend it downward so the wires are parallel **(c)**.

4 Following the **Template**, use your thumb to gently shape the longer wire to mimic the shape of the shorter wire, leaving about 2 mm between the wires. Using roundnose pliers, grasp the end of the longer wire, and make a spiral going in the opposite direction of the first spiral.

Repeat steps 1–4 to make a second frame that mirrors the first.

Use a chasing hammer and bench block to hammer the frames. Do not hammer the top loop; doing so will distort the shape and possibly break the wire **(d)**.

Embellishment

5 Cut 2¼ in. (57 mm) of 22-gauge (0.64 mm) square wire, and twist it (Basics, p. 109). Use roundnose pliers to make a tiny loop at one end of the wire, then start to make an open spiral (Basics, p. 109). Fit the tiny loop in the center of the spiral in the shorter wire of one frame, and use your fingers to guide the twisted wire to match the shape of the spiral.

Mark where the twisted wire meets the top frame loop. Add 3 mm (⅛ in.) and cut the wire. Make a tiny loop facing away from the frame **(e)**.

6 To make the twisted wire embellishment for the longer spiral, repeat step 5 with 3¼ in. (83 mm) of wire **(f)**.

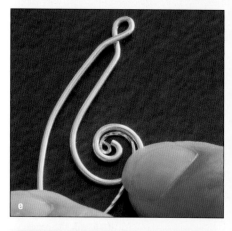

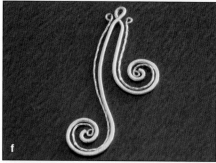

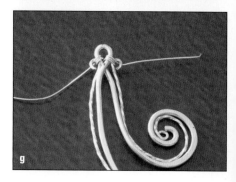

Process photos by Erin Paton.

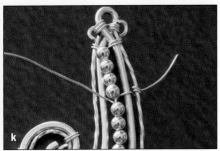

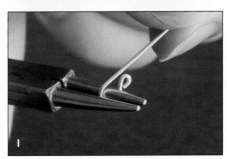

7 Cut 4 in. (10.2 cm) of 28-gauge (0.32 mm) wrapping wire. You'll use this gauge for wrapping wire throughout the rest of the project.

Use the wrapping wire to make three wraps to attach the frame's top loop and a tiny twisted-wire loop. Thread the wrapping wire through the top loop, and make three wraps to attach the frame and the remaining tiny twisted-wire loop. Using flush cutters, trim the wrapping wire at the back of the frame. Use bentnose pliers to flatten the wrapping-wire tails against the frame **(g)**.

8 Cut 7 in. (17.8 cm) of wrapping wire, and make two wraps at each of the five connection points to attach the twisted wires to the frame. After you trim each tail at the back of the frame, flatten the tail. Use nylon-jaw pliers to gently squeeze each set of wraps to lock it in place **(h)**.

9 Cut 12 in. (30.5 cm) of wrapping wire. At the top of the shorter frame wire, make two wraps around the twisted wire and the frame. Thread the wire under the opposite side, and make two wraps around the longer frame and twisted wire. Use flatnose pliers to bend the wrapping wire down between the frame wires.

String 12 2 mm beads on the wrapping wire, and guide them down along the longer frame wire. Snug up the beads, and make two wraps around the longer frame and twisted wire **(i)**.

10 String a 2 mm bead, and make two wraps around the frame only. String a 2 mm bead, and make three wraps around the frame only.

String a 2 mm bead, and make three wraps around the frame and twisted wire.

String a 2 mm bead, and make four wraps around the frame only.

String a 2 mm bead, and make four wraps around the frame only.

String a 3 mm bead, and make five wraps around the frame only.

String a 4 mm bead, make three wraps around the frame only, then trim and flatten the wire **(j)**.

11 To add a brace through the middle of the earring, cut 3 in. (76 mm) of wrapping wire. Count down four beads from the top of the earring, and make two wraps around one of the twisted wires adjacent to the fourth bead. Wrap over the adjacent frame wire, then make one wrap around the wire underneath the fourth bead. Take the wire under the next frame wire and make one wrap. Then make two wraps around the remaining twisted wire. Trim and flatten the wire **(k)**.

Repeat steps 5–11 for the other earring.

Ear wires

12 Cut 2¾ in. (70 mm) of 20-gauge (0.81 mm) wire. Using roundnose pliers, make a small loop at one end. Grasp the wire adjacent to the loop, and bend the wire in the opposite direction of the loop to make a U shape about 3 mm (⅛ in.) in diameter **(l)**.

13 Bend the wire tail around a ring mandrel at size U.S. 0.75–1. Use your flatnose pliers to bend the end of the wire up slightly. Cut the wire 5 mm (³⁄₁₆ in.) from the bend. Hammer the U bend and the 5 mm (³⁄₁₆-in.) tail. Use a cup bur and/or sandpaper to smooth the end of the ear wire. Open the loop of the ear wire, slide on the earring's top loop, and close the loop **(m)**. Repeat for the other earring.

TIP

To finish a wire tail so it won't stick out, grasp it with bentnose pliers while pulling and bending it up 90 degrees. Cut the tail with flush cutters at the back, center of the frame. Then use bentnose pliers to firmly flatten the end.

Curlicue lace earrings

Use only basic hand tools to make lightweight, freeform earrings that look like fine jewelry.

by Melody MacDuffee

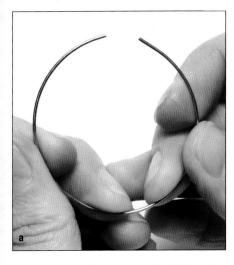

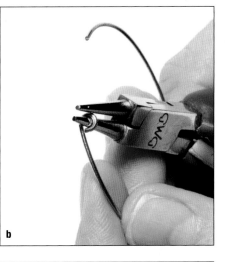

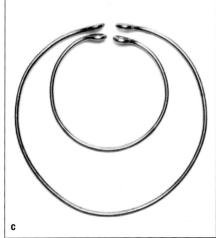

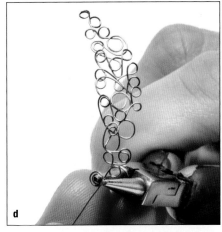

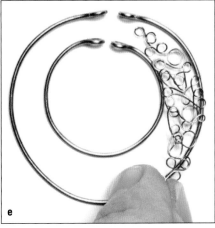

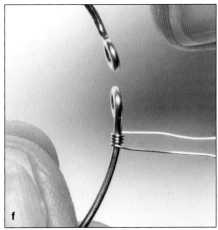

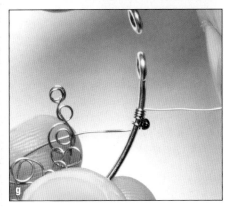

Hoops

1 Flush-cut a 5½-in. (14 cm) and a 3½-in. (8.9 cm) piece of 18-gauge wire. Form each into a round hoop around a mandrel or by gradually shaping them with your hands **(a)**.

2 Make a plain loop (Basics, p. 110) on both ends of each wire **(b)**. The loops should be formed in the same direction, toward your work surface. Lay the small hoop inside the large hoop to test the spacing **(c)**.

Looking for color contrast or more beads? As you make the curlicue lace in step 3, add a Charlotte to every or every other loop, or use multiple colors of Charlottes.

Curlicue lace

3 Cut 1 yd. (91.4 cm) of 26-gauge wire. Using roundnose pliers, make small loops and spirals in the wire, first in one direction and then in the other, to create a strip of curlicue lace **(d)**. Gradually

increase the size and complexity of the loops and spirals to increase the width of the strip. Lay the strip between the two hoops occasionally to make sure it is the right size and shape **(e)**. Continue until you have used the entire length of wire. If necessary, cut a new piece, and continue shaping the wire until you have enough curlicue lace to fill the space between the hoops.

Wire wrapping

4 Cut a 24-in. (61 cm) piece of 28-gauge wire. Leaving a 1-in. (25.5 mm) tail, make several tight wraps around the larger hoop just below one plain loop **(f)**. After the third wrap, string a 13º Charlotte, and position it against the outside of the hoop **(g)**.

5 Set the curlicue lace inside the large hoop. Continue to wrap the 28-gauge wire around the hoop, adding a Charlotte after every third wrap. At each point where the curlicue lace comes in contact with the hoop, wrap the wire through the

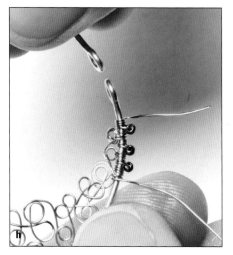

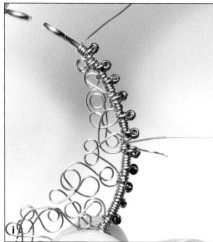

materials

Earrings 1¾ in. (44 mm)

- Craft wire, round, dead soft (Parawire, gold; www.parawire.com):
- 18 in. (45.7 cm) 18-gauge (1.0 mm)
- 2–3 yd. (1.8–2.7 m) 26-gauge (0.4 mm)
- 8–9 ft. (2.4–2.7 m) 28-gauge (0.32 mm)
- 1 g 13º Charlottes
- 2 18-gauge (1.0 mm) jump rings, 6 mm inner diameter (ID)
- Pair of ear wires

tools & supplies

- 2 pairs of chainnose, flatnose, and/or bentnose pliers
- Roundnose pliers
- Flush cutters strong enough to cut 18-gauge (1.0 mm) wire
- Round mandrels (optional)

lace strip to anchor it **(h)**. Make sure the wraps are tight around the hoop and pushed snugly up against each other. Also ensure that the lace is distributed evenly around the inside of the hoop.

TIP

If desired, tack your lace strip to the large hoop with scraps of 28-gauge wire to keep it in place before starting the final wrapping.

6 If you run out of wire, leave a short tail sticking out from the hoop. Cut a new piece of 28-gauge wire, and continue wrapping around the hoop **(i)**. Once you reach the other end of the hoop, make several wraps, and trim and tuck the wire (Basics, p. 109). Go back to each place where you added new wire, and trim and tuck each wire tail.

7 Cut a new 24-in. (61 cm) piece of 28-gauge wire. Set the small hoop inside the large hoop, and repeat the wrapping process along the inside edge of the lace strip, omitting the Charlottes **(j)**. Gently push or pull the lace strip into the proper shape if it is too wide or too narrow to fill the space between the hoops. Again, take care that the lace is distributed evenly around the hoop. The

earring may gradually take on a slightly convex shape. If your wrapping leaves any section bare, simply make a small piece of lace the size and shape of the unfilled area and fill in the gap, making sure that it is set against lace that is already secure **(k)**.

8 Open a 6 mm jump ring (Basics, p. 110). Attach all four plain loops and the loop of an ear wire **(l)**. Close the jump ring.

9 Repeat steps 1–8 to make a second earring.

3-D earrings

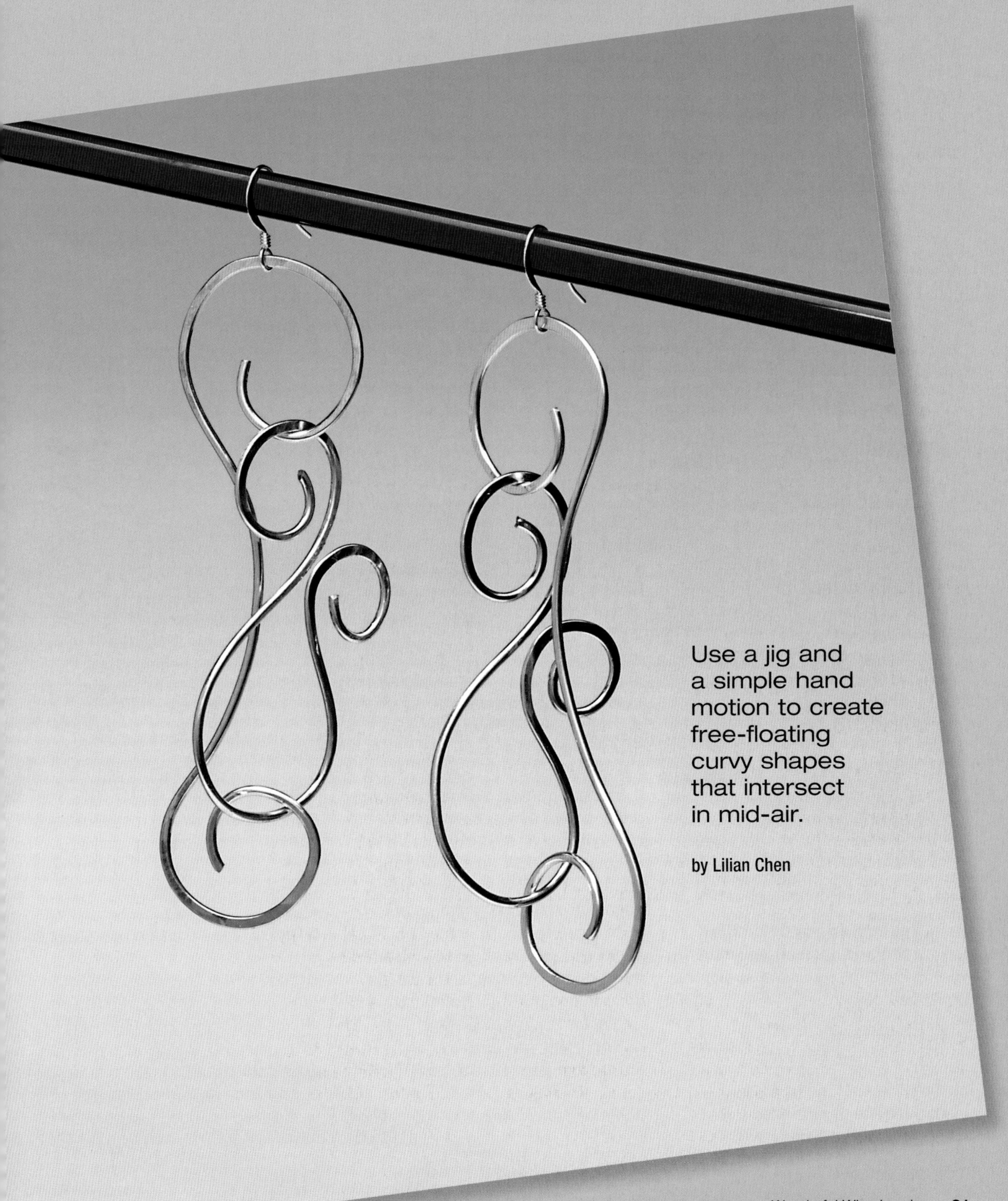

Use a jig and
a simple hand
motion to create
free-floating
curvy shapes
that intersect
in mid-air.

by Lilian Chen

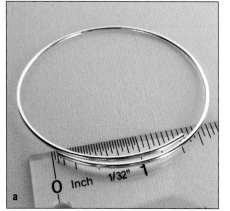

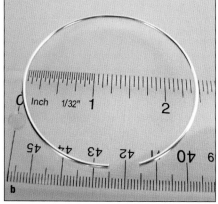

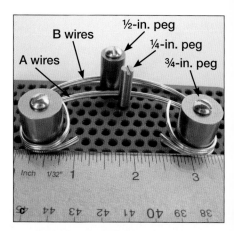

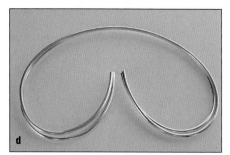

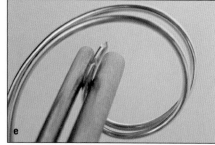

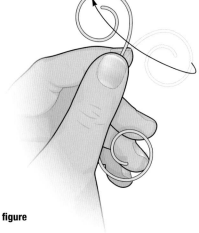

materials

Earrings 4 in. (10.2 cm)

- 14-gauge (1.6 mm) silver-plated tarnish-resistant Artistic Wire
- Pair of ear wires

tools & supplies

- 2 pairs of chainnose, flatnose, and/or bentnose pliers
- Roundnose pliers
- Flush cutters strong enough to cut 14-gauge (1.6 mm) wire, or memory wire cutters
- Now That's a Jig! with ¾-in. (19 mm), ½-in. (13 mm), and ¼-in. (6.5 mm) pegs (www.now-thats-a-jig.com)
- Steel bench block or anvil
- Utility hammer

TIP

Do not straighten any of the wire for the earrings. Instead, allow the wire to keep the natural shape of the packaged coil.

1 Flush-cut a piece of 14-gauge wire from the coil so that the ends overlap about 1½ in. (38 mm) **(a)**. Flush-cut a second piece of wire in the same manner. These will be your A wires.

2 Flush-cut a piece of 14-gauge wire from the coil so that there is a ⅜-in. (9.5 mm) gap between the ends **(b)**. Flush-cut a second piece of wire in the same manner. These will be your B wires.

3 Arrange two ¾-in. (19 mm) pegs, one ½-in. (13 mm) peg, and one ¼-in. (6.5 mm) peg on the Now That's a Jig! as shown **(c)**. From the outer edge of one ¾-in. (19 mm) peg to the outer edge of the other should measure approximately 3 in. (76 mm). Still referring to **(c)**, center the B wires around the ½-in. (13 mm) peg, and bring the ends around the ¾-in. (19 mm) pegs. Center the A wires around the ¼-in. (6.5 mm) peg, and bring the ends around the ¾-in. (19 mm) pegs.

4 Remove the A wires from the jig bed **(d)**. Working with both A wires together,

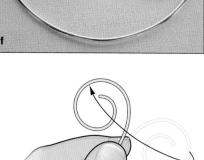

figure

grasp one end with roundnose pliers, and pull inward, creating a more pronounced curl **(e)**. Repeat with the other end of the A wires **(f)**.

5 Repeat step 4 with the B wires **(g)**.

6 Working with one B wire at a time, grasp the wire with your hand so that the top curl is exposed. Using any hand movement that is comfortable for you, twist the top curl so that it is facing opposite the bottom curl **(figure)**. This B wire should now look like the bottom wire in **(h)**. Turn the wire, and repeat

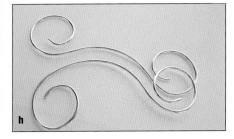

h

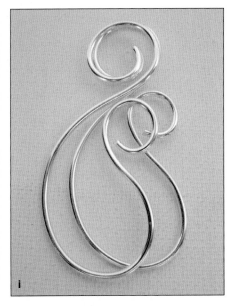

i

j

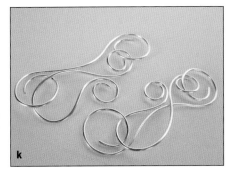

k

this step with the other curled end. Both curls should be facing the same direction, and there should be a slight "bump" at the center of the wire, as in the top wire in **(h)**.

- String beads or crystals onto the A wires in step 4, after removing the wire from the jig bed but before shaping the curl.

- Glue flat-back crystals to the ends of the A and B wires.

- Create a smaller curl on one end of the A wires; orient the smaller curl either at the top or bottom of the earring for different effects.

- Change the orientation of the B wires (hang them upside down).

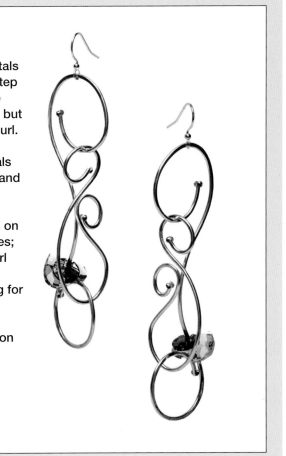

7 Repeat step 6 with the other B wire. Make sure that both B wires have the same shape.

8 Working with both B wires together, press the "bumps" against a ¾-in. (19 mm) peg on the jig to create a stylized S-shape **(i)**.

TIP
Push the wire little by little around the peg to get a smooth shape.

9 Repeat step 6 with the A wires, making sure the A wires are longer than the B wires **(j)**.

10 Slide the top and bottom of a B wire through the curls of an A wire, and make sure that the B wire hangs freely when the A wire is suspended. Adjust the wires as needed. Repeat with the other set of A and B wires **(k)**.

11 Disassemble the pieces, place each A and B wire on a bench block, and hammer to flatten and work-harden the pieces. Reassemble both sets of A and B wires.

12 Open the loop of an ear wire (Basics, p. 110), attach it to the top of an A wire, and close the loop. Repeat for the other earring, creating a mirror image of the first earring. Make sure that the ear wires can't slide off the ends of the A wires. If they do, flair the ends of the A wires some more with the hammer.

Copper ring trio

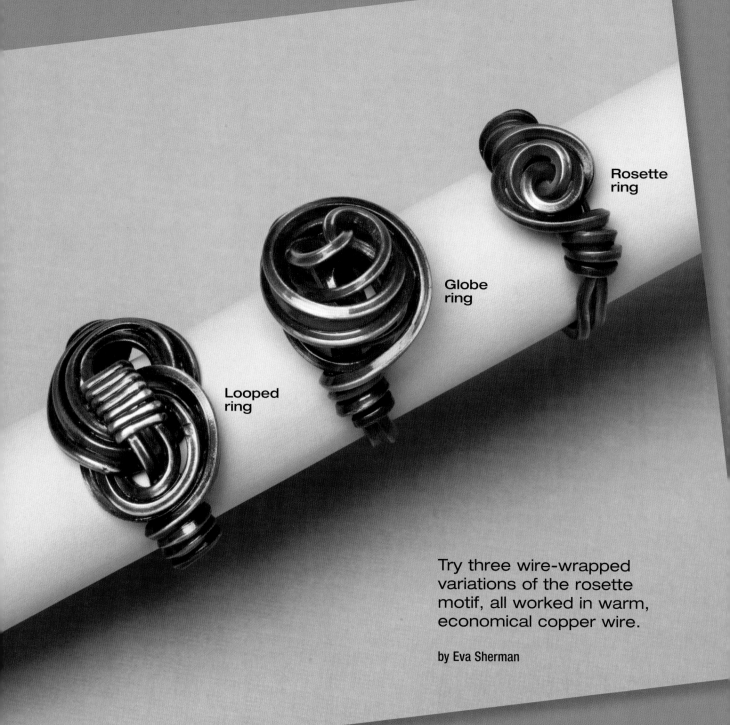

Rosette ring

Globe ring

Looped ring

Try three wire-wrapped variations of the rosette motif, all worked in warm, economical copper wire.

by Eva Sherman

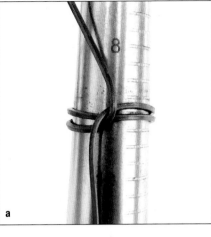

a

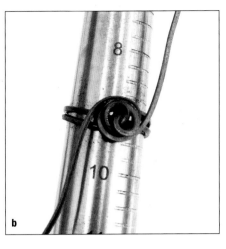

b

c

d

Before creating the rings, anneal the wire by heating it with a butane torch until it glows and then quenching it in water.

Rosette ring

1 Cut 2 ft. (61 cm) of 16-gauge square wire, and center it on a ring mandrel at two sizes larger than the desired finished size. Wrap one full rotation, and tightly twist the ends together once **(a)**.

2 Windmill the ends around the center until the rosette is the desired size. Trim the ends to 2 in. (51 mm) **(b)**.

3 Remove the ring from the mandrel, and wrap each end around the band two or three times **(c)**.

TIP

Remove the ring from the mandrel as directed. For clarity, the ring may still appear on the mandrel in the photos.

4 Trim each end on the outside of the band. Using chainnose pliers, gently squeeze the wraps in place **(d)**.

5 On a bench block, hammer the ring band with a rubber mallet to work-harden. Pickle the piece (Basics, p. 109) to remove fire-scale, and polish with a brass brush. If desired, patinate the piece with liver of sulfur (Basics, p. 110), and apply a coat of spray enamel to seal and protect.

materials

Rosette ring
- 2 ft. (61 cm) 16-gauge (1.3 mm) copper wire, square, dead soft

Globe ring
- 2 ft. (61 cm) 16-gauge (1.3 mm) copper wire, square, dead soft

Looped ring
- 2 ft. (61 cm) 16-gauge (1.3 mm) copper wire, square, dead soft
- 6 in. (15 cm) 18-gauge (1.0 mm) copper wire, half round, dead soft or annealed

tools & supplies

- Chainnose pliers
- Flush cutters strong enough to cut 16-gauge (1.3 mm) wire
- Butane torch
- Ring mandrel
- Steel bench block or anvil
- Rubber mallet
- Pickle and pickle pot, such as a Crock-Pot or container on a hot plate
- Brass brush or fine steel wool
- Liver of sulfur (optional)
- Spray enamel (optional)

e

f

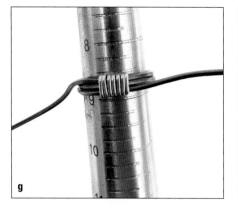

Globe ring

1 Repeat step 1 of the "Rosette ring."

2 Tightly twist the ends together two more times **(e)**, and windmill the ends around the center, working down toward the band, until the globe is the desired size **(f)**. Trim the ends to 2 in. (51 mm).

3 Repeat steps 3–5 of "Rosette ring."

Looped ring

1 Repeat step 1 of "Rosette ring," but do not twist the ends together.

2 Remove the ring from the mandrel, and wrap a 6-in. (15.2 cm) piece of 18-gauge wire seven times around the center of the band. Trim each end of the wire on the outside of the band. Using chainnose pliers, gently squeeze the wraps in place **(g)**.

3 Loop one wire end around the outer edge and back under the center. Repeat with the other wire end, making sure to insert the wire through the first loop **(h)**. Repeat two times on each side.

4 Trim both ends to 2 in. (51 mm), and wrap each end around the band three times.

5 Repeat steps 4 and 5 of "Rosette ring" **(i)**.

Wired steampunk rings

Wire together a mix
of gears, findings,
and crystals to form
steampunk-inspired rings.

by Irina Miech

materials

Ring, adjustable size
- Sterling silver wire:
  24-gauge (0.51 mm),
  round, dead-soft, 24 in.
  (61.0 cm)
- 12 mm Swarovski
  Elements #1122 rivoli
- 25 mm bronze gear
  finding with large
  center opening
- 10-loop round filigree
  finding
- 55 mm ring shank

Crystal gear variation
- Gunmetal wire: 28-gauge
  (0.32 mm), 20 in.
  (50.8 cm)
- 14 mm Swarovski
  crystal ring
- 19 mm gear finding
- 21 mm sprocket

Filigree bird variation
- Gunmetal wire: 28-gauge
  (0.32 mm), 20 in.
  (50.8 cm)
- 15 x 20 mm brass filigree
  bird component
- 21 mm sprocket
- 19 mm sprocket

tools & supplies
- Wirework toolbox, p. 105
- Ring mandrel

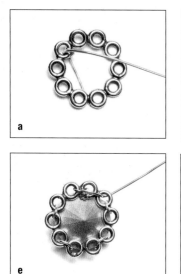

a

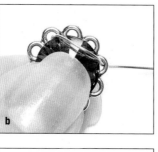

b

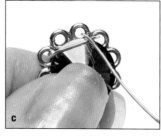

c

d

e

f

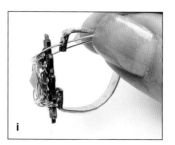

g

h

i

j

Ring

1 Cut a 10-in. (25.4 cm) piece of 24-gauge (0.51 mm) wire, and wrap it twice around loop 1 (on the inside of the loop) of a 10-loop round filigree component **(a)**.

2 Center a 12 mm rivoli on top of the filigree component. Skipping two loops, thread the wire through loop 4 of the filigree component, front to back, crossing over the rivoli along the edge **(b)**. Thread the wire through loop 3, back to front **(c)**.

3 Repeat step 2 until you have gone all the way around the filigree component, creating a pentagon. At this point the rivoli should be securely anchored in place **(d)**.

4 On the back of the filigree component, thread the wire from loop 2 to loop 10, back to front **(e)**. Skipping two of the loops, thread the wire through loop 3, front to back, so that it sits behind the rivoli along the edge.

5 Thread the wire through loop 2, back to front. Repeat step 2 until you have completed another pentagon on the back of the rivoli. The

wire should end toward the back.

Secure the wire by wrapping it tightly around one of the loops on the inner circle of the component. Trim excess wire. Use chainnose pliers to pinch the wire in place **(f)**.

6 Stack the wired rivoli on top of a gear finding. Cut a 4-in. (10.2 cm) piece of 24-gauge (0.51 mm) wire, and wrap three times through one of the loops of the 10-loop finding and around the brass gear between two of the spokes. Create a second wrap through the loop and gear components directly across from the first wrap **(g)**.

7 Shape a ring-shank finding around a ring mandrel. Use chainnose pliers to bend the ends inward **(h)**.

8 Cut 2–3 in. (51–76 mm) of 24-gauge (0.51 mm) wire, and attach the wrapped component to the ring shank through the holes at each end of the shank **(i)**. Wrap the wire around the shank **(j)** and trim any wire.

Crystal gear and filigree bird variations

9 Crystal gear: Cut two 5-in. (12.7 cm) pieces of 28-gauge (0.32 mm) gunmetal wire. Starting in the center of one of the wire pieces, wrap around both the crystal ring and gear three times, positioning the wire between the cogs of the gear finding. Repeat on the opposite side.

10 Filigree bird: Cut two 5-in. (12.7 cm) pieces of 28-gauge (0.32 mm) gunmetal wire. Starting at the center of the wire, wrap around the edge of the bird finding and through the cogs of the gear. Repeat on the opposite side.

11 For both variations: Use the remaining wire ends to securely wrap the bird and gear component on top of the sprocket.

12 For both variations: Wrap the ends around another wire on the back of the piece, and tuck in toward the front. Repeat steps 7 and 8.

Swaying frame earrings

Swarovski sew-on stones swing in the breeze with these easy wire frames. Meanwhile, decorative wraps and chain dangles draw the eye down past every elegant inch of the design.

by Melissa Grakowsky Shippee

materials

Earrings 3½ in. (89 mm)

- Nontarnish copper wire, round (vintage bronze):
  - 16 in. (40.6 cm) 18-gauge (1.0 mm)
  - 88 in. (2.2 m) 24-gauge (0.5 mm)
- 2 9 x 18 mm space-cut sew-on stones (Swarovski #3251, crystal bronze shade)
- 12 in. (30.5 cm) 2 x 3 mm cable chain (antique copper)
- Pair of ear wires (vintage bronze)

tools & supplies

- 2 pairs of chainnose pliers
- Nylon-jaw pliers
- Roundnose pliers
- Wire cutters
- Steel bench block or anvil
- Hammer
- Tape

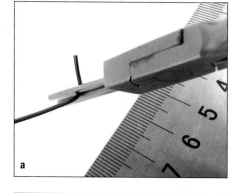

a

b

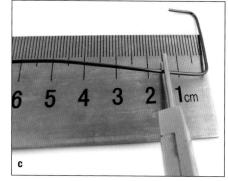

c

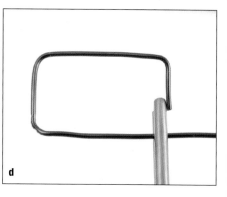

d

Earring frame

1 Keeping the wire on the spool, use nylon-jaw pliers to straighten approximately 8 in. (20.3 cm) of 18-gauge wire.

2 Using roundnose pliers, grasp the wire ⅜ in. (9.5 mm) from the end of the wire, and make a 90-degree bend to form a soft corner **(a)**.

3 Form another soft corner approximately ¹³⁄₁₆ in. (21 mm) from the previous corner **(b)**.

4 Form another soft corner about ⅝ in. (16 mm) from the previous corner **(c)**.

5 Repeat step 3 to form the last soft corner **(d)**.

6 Trim the overlapping wire in the middle of the short side of the frame **(e)**. This side of the frame will be slightly shorter than the opposite side and will be the top of the frame.

7 Place the frame on a bench block, and hammer it to flatten and work-harden it **(f)**.

e

f

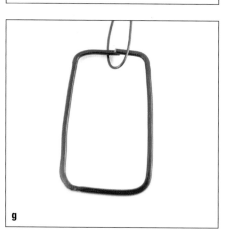

g

h

8 Cut two 8-in. (20.3 cm) pieces of 24-gauge (wrapping) wire.

9 Bend one wire in half over the top of the frame where the ends meet **(g)**. Hold the ends in place while you wrap half of the 8-in. (20.3 cm) wire toward one

corner. Repeat with the other half of the wire, wrapping toward the other corner. Trim and tuck the ends of the wire on the back of the frame (Basics, p. 109).

10 Work as in step 9 to wrap the bottom of the frame **(h)**.

i

j

k

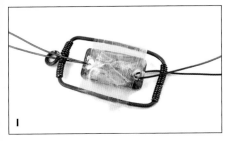

l

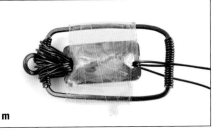

m

n

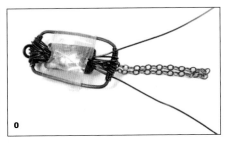

o

p

Sew-on stone

11 Using roundnose pliers, make a 2 mm loop at the end of the 18-gauge wire on the spool. Trim the loop flush with the end of the wire, creating a jump ring **(i)**.

12 Place the jump ring on a bench block, and hammer it to flatten and work-harden it **(j)**. Close the jump ring completely.

13 Tape a 9 x 18 mm space-cut sew-on stone in the center of the frame, leaving the holes of the stone exposed **(k)**. Make sure the stone is slightly closer to the top of the frame than the bottom and that the trimmed wrapping wires are positioned at the back of the frame.

TIP

If your stone has foiling on the back, do not tape the foiling.

14 Cut two 14-in. (35.6 cm) pieces of wrapping wire. Insert one wire through the top hole of the stone, and bend the wire in half. String the 2 mm jump ring over both ends of the wire, and center the jump ring at the top of the frame **(l)**.

15 Wrap one end of the wire around the frame, through the top hole of the stone, and back up through the jump ring. Make two more wraps through the jump ring and the stone, and then make three or four wraps just through the stone and around the frame, working toward the corner. Repeat this step with the other half of the wire. Trim and tuck both ends close to the hole of the stone at the back of the frame **(m)**.

TIP

Hold the stone firmly in place while you wrap so it does not shift position in the frame. You can also use the second wire from step 14 to begin wrapping the other end of the stone, as shown in (l) and (m), to help stabilize the stone.

16 Insert the other wrapping wire through the bottom hole of the stone, and bend the wire in half. With each end of the wire, make a few wraps through the hole of the stone and around the bottom of the frame.

17 Cut four 1½-in. (38 mm) pieces of chain. String a chain on each end of the wire, and position them along the bottom of the frame **(n)**.

18 Wrap one end of the wire around the bottom of the frame, up through the hole of the stone, down through the chain, around the bottom of the frame, and up through the stone. Then bring the wire down to the bottom of the frame. Repeat this step with the other wire and chain **(o)**.

19 On each end of the wire, string another chain, and continue as before, working toward each corner. Make two more wraps through the stone and around the frame without going through any chains. Trim and tuck both ends close to the hole of the stone at the back of the frame.

20 Remove the tape. Open the loop of an ear wire (Basics, p. 110), and attach the jump ring at the top of the frame. Close the loop **(p)**.

21 Make a second earring.

Scrollwork earrings

Use simple wirework to make delicate Victorian-style earrings with a lot of charm.

by Colette Kimon

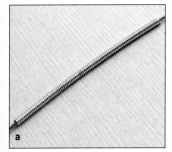

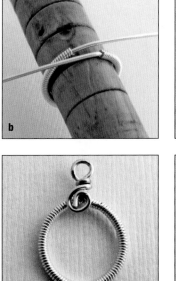

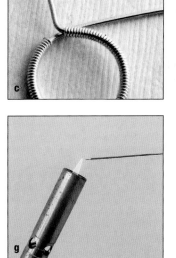

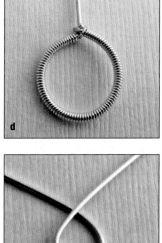

Coiled frame

1 Cut a 4-in. (10.2 cm) piece of 20-gauge sterling silver (core) wire. Using a fine-tip permanent marker, mark 1 in. (25.5 mm) from the end of the wire.

2 Cut a 20-in. (50.8 cm) piece of 26-gauge (wrapping) wire. Starting at the 1-in. (25.5 mm) mark, coil the wrapping wire around the core wire (Basics, p. 109) until you have a 1½-in. (38 mm) coil. You should have 1 in. (25.5 mm) of bare core wire on one end and 1½ in.

(38 mm) on the other. Trim and tuck the ends of the wrapping wire (Basics, p. 109) **(a)**.

3 Form the coiled section of the core wire around a ½-in. (13 mm) mandrel so that both ends of the coil meet. Cross the shorter end of bare wire behind the longer end **(b)**. Carefully remove the wire from the mandrel.

4 With the tip of your chainnose pliers, grasp the longer end of the bare wire

TIP

In step 2, you can use a drill to make the coiled section of the core more quickly. Secure the wrapping wire to one end of the core wire with some painter's tape. Insert the end of the core wire into the chuck of the drill, and slowly spin the drill to coil the wire. When you are finished, remove the tape, and arrange the coil as directed.

next to the coil, and bend it up at a 90-degree angle **(c)**.

5 With the shorter end of the bare wire, make a full wrap around the longer end, close to the 90-degree bend. Trim and tuck the shorter end of the bare wire **(d)**. If necessary, place the wire back on the mandrel to adjust the shape.

6 Make a wrapped loop (Basics, p. 110) above the wrap from step 5, and trim the wire to ½ in. (13 mm) **(e)**. Form an open spiral (Basics, p. 109) with the wire, and center the spiral under the wrapped loop **(f)**.

7 Repeat steps 1–6 to make a second coiled frame, and set the frames aside.

Scrollwork

8 Cut a 6½-in. (16.5 cm) piece of 20-gauge fine-silver wire. Grasp the wire with

tweezers, and use a butane torch to ball up each end of the wire **(g)**. After balling, the wire should measure approximately 6 in. (15.2 cm).

TIP

Watch a video tutorial on balling the end of a wire at www.ArtJewelryMag.com/ videos. If you'd prefer not to ball the ends, cut your wire to just 6 in. (15.2 cm).

9 With the largest part of your roundnose pliers, grasp the midpoint of the wire, and cross the ends to form a loop **(h)**. This will be the center loop of the scrollwork.

10 About 1 mm from the largest part of your roundnose pliers, lightly grasp the wire to the left of the center loop. Form the wire around the pliers counterclockwise, creating a slightly smaller second loop **(i)**.

materials

Earrings 1½ in. (38 mm)
- Fine-silver wire, round, dead soft:
  - 13 in. (33 cm) 20-gauge (0.8 mm)
  - 6 ft. (1.8 m) 26-gauge (0.4 mm)
- 11 in. (27.9 cm) 20-gauge (0.8 mm) sterling silver wire, round, dead soft
- 6 2.5 mm sterling silver seamless round beads

tools & supplies

- Wirework toolbox, p. 105
- Fine-tip permanent marker
- ½-in. (13 mm) mandrel
- Tweezers
- Butane torch
- Liver of sulfur (optional)
- Tumbler with steel shot and burnishing compound (optional)

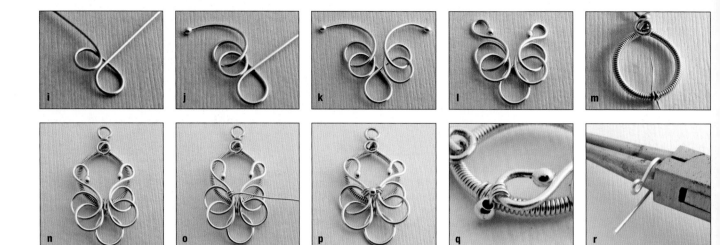

11 With your roundnose pliers, grasp the end of the wire, and curve it loosely in the same direction as the previous loop. Work slowly to form a large third loop, curving small sections at a time and threading the end of the wire through the second loop. Reposition your pliers inside the third loop, and keep curving and pushing the wire through the second loop until the third loop is about the same size as the second loop. The wire end should be approximately ¾ in. (19 mm) long **(j)**.

12 Repeat steps 10 and 11 on the right side of the center loop **(k)**.

13 On each end of the wire below the balled up tip, use roundnose pliers to make a loop toward the center of the scrollwork. Adjust any of the loops as necessary to compress the scrollwork and make it symmetrical **(l)**.

14 Repeat steps 8–13 to make a second scrollwork piece.

Assembly

15 Using a fine-tip permanent marker, mark the bottom center of one of the coiled frames. Cut a 6-in. (15.2 cm) piece of 26-gauge (wrapping) wire. Leaving a ½-in. (13 mm) tail, make three wraps around the frame at the mark **(m)**.

16 Position one of the scrollwork pieces above the coiled frame, with the top of the center loop directly above the wrapped mark on the frame. Make three wraps around the frame and through the center loop to connect the two pieces **(n)**. Trim and tuck the ends of the wrapping wire at the back of the scrollwork.

17 Cut a 4-in. (10.2 cm) piece of wrapping wire. Locate the point where the wire of the third loop on the left side of the scrollwork crosses itself, and make three wraps around both wires **(o)**. Wrap from left to right so that the working wire is on top when you are done with your wraps. String a 2.5 mm bead on the wire, and wrap around both wires where the third loop on the right crosses itself **(p)**. Trim and tuck the ends of the wrapping wire at the back of the scrollwork.

18 Cut a 3-in. (76 mm) piece of wrapping wire. Make three wraps around the last loop on the top left side of the scrollwork and the coiled frame. String a 2.5 mm bead on the wire, and make three wraps around the frame only. The bead should be positioned on the coiled frame directly above the last loop **(q)**. Repeat this step on the other side of the scrollwork. Trim and tuck the ends of the wrapping wire.

19 Repeat steps 15–18 to assemble the other coiled frame and scrollwork.

Ear wires

20 Cut a 1½-in. (38 mm) piece of 20-gauge sterling silver wire. Use a flat needle file to flatten and smooth one end. With the tip of your roundnose pliers, make a loop at this end. Mark the wire ½ in. (13 mm) from the base of the loop, and grasp the mark with the largest part of your roundnose pliers. Form the wire into a hook around the jaw of the pliers, bending the wire away from the loop **(r)**.

21 Flush-cut the tip of the ear wire at a 45-degree angle, and then use a needle file or sandpaper to smooth any sharpness or rough edges. With the largest part of your roundnose pliers, grasp the tip of the ear wire, and bend it slightly outward.

22 Repeat steps 20 and 21 to make a second ear wire.

23 Open the loop of each ear wire (Basics, p. 110). For each earring, attach the wrapped loop at the top of a coiled frame, and close the loop. If desired, use liver of sulfur to patinate (Basics, p. 110) the earrings, and then tumble-polish them (Basics, p. 110).

Leaf drop earrings

A marquise-shaped frame is the base for this elegant, leaf-inspired earring design. Faceted bead embellishment adds color, texture, and sparkle.

by Lisa Claxton

materials

Pair of earrings

- Sterling silver or fine-silver wire: 26-gauge (0.40 mm), round, dead-soft, 6 ft. (1.8 m)
- 2 12 x 29 mm marquise-shaped soldered jump rings
- **30** 3–4 mm faceted beads
- **2** spacers
- **2** 1½-in. (13 mm) 24-gauge (0.51 mm) head pins
- pair of earring findings

tools & supplies

- Wirework toolbox, p. 105

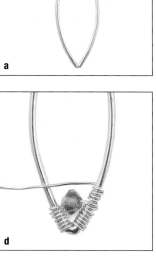

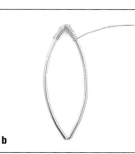

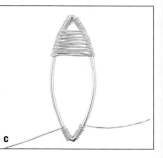

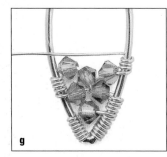

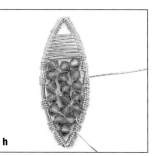

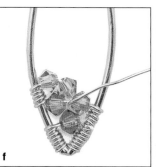

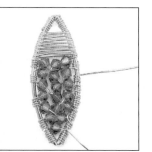

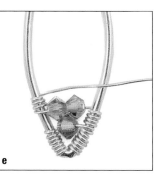

1 Cut a 12-in. (30.5 cm) piece of 26-gauge (0.40 mm) wrapping wire. Leaving a short tail, make eight wraps around a marquise frame on one side near its top point **(a)**.

2 Skip the top point, and make eight wraps on the opposite side of the frame. Tighten the wraps on both sides so there are no gaps. Flush cut the short tail on the inside of the frame **(b)**.

3 Pull the wire across the back of the frame, and make one wrap around the opposite side. Pull the wire across the front of the frame, and make one wrap around the opposite side. While wrapping, hold the wire in place with your thumb.

4 Repeat step 3 until the wire crosses eight times over the front and back of the frame. Then, make one more wrap around one side of the frame, and cut the wire flush against the inside of the frame.

5 Cut a 12-in. (30.5 cm) piece of wrapping wire. Leaving a short tail, make seven wraps on each side of the frame's bottom point **(c)**.

6 String a bead on the wrapping wire, and make four wraps on the opposite side of the frame **(d)**.

7 String two beads on the wire, and make four wraps on the opposite side of the frame **(e)**.

8 String two beads, and make one wrap between the last two beads added **(f)**. String one bead, and make four wraps on the opposite side of the frame **(g)**.

9 Repeat step 8 until the beads fill the frame. To finish, wrap the frame until the wraps rest against the wire cap. Cut the wire flush against the inside of the frame.

10 Cut a 12-in. (30.5 cm) piece of wrapping wire and make tight wraps all the way up one side of the exposed frame, starting at the first gap at the bottom of the frame. Either skip the existing wraps by threading the wire alongside them on the inside of the frame **(h)** or wrap between them. Then, cut the wrapping wire flush against the inside of the frame. Repeat to wrap the opposite side **(i)**.

11 Attach an ear wire to the top of the frame. On a head pin, string a 3 mm bead and a spacer, and make the first half of a wrapped loop (Basics, p. 110). Attach the loop to the bottom of a frame, and complete the wraps. Repeat the steps to make a second earring.

    To use this component as a pendant instead of an earring, attach a jump ring to the top instead of an ear wire.

Riveting spirals set

This easy introduction to riveting uses two-part rivets. Once you've made your wire spirals, layer them with metal components and rivet them together!

by Irina Miech

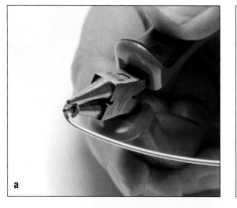

a

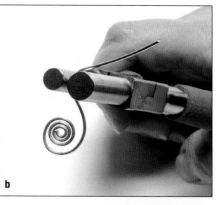

b

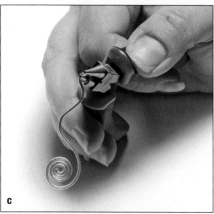

c

d

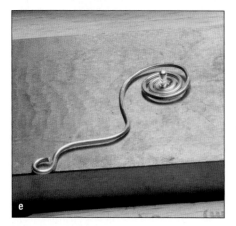

e

f

5 Cut a 3-in. (76 mm) piece of 24-gauge (wrapping) wire. Make a tight three-wrap coil around the component below the zigzag. Then wrap around the zigzag portion of the component, spacing out the wraps, and finish with another tight three-wrap coil above the zigzag. Trim and tuck the wrapping wire (Basics, p. 109).

6 Attach an ear wire to the loop at the top of the component.

7 Repeat steps 1–6 to make a second earring, forming it so that it creates a mirror image of the first.

Spiral earrings

1 Flush-cut a 5-in. (12.7 cm) piece of 18-gauge wire. Using roundnose pliers, make a loop approximately ⅛ in. (3 mm) wide at the end of the wire **(a)**. Form a spiral (Basics, p. 109) around the loop; let the spiral open after the third turn.

2 Using large bail-making pliers, create a soft zigzag in the straight tail of the wire **(b)** so that the component (including the spiral) measures approximately 1½ in. (38 mm) long. Using roundnose pliers, make a loop at the end of the zigzag **(c)**.

3 Place the component on a bench block, and lightly hammer it with a chasing hammer to flatten and work-harden it **(d)**.

4 Place the bottom half of a rivet on the bench block. Place the component over the rivet half so that the rivet protrudes through the center of the spiral **(e)**. Then place a flat spacer on the rivet, over the center of the spiral **(f)**. Set the top half of the rivet in place, and carefully hammer with a riveting hammer until the rivet holds firmly.

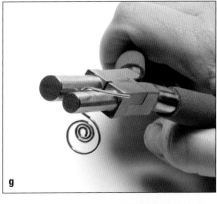

g

h

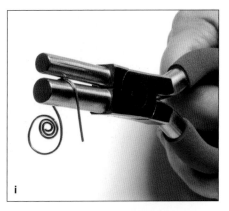

i

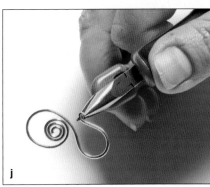

j

k

l

Spiral bracelet

1 Flush-cut a 4-in. (10.2 cm) piece of 18-gauge wire. Using roundnose pliers, make a loop approximately ⅛ in. (3 mm) wide at the end of the wire. Form a spiral (Basics, p. 109) around the loop; let the spiral open after the third turn.

2 Using medium bail-making pliers, create a soft zigzag **(g)** so that the component (including the spiral) measures approximately ⅞ in. (22 mm). Using roundnose pliers, make a loop at the end of the zigzag **(h)**.

3 Repeat steps 1 and 2 to create four additional components. Try to make them consistent in size and shape.

4 To make the hook of the clasp, repeat step 1 using approximately 5 in. (12.7 cm) of 18-gauge wire, and then use medium bail-making pliers to create a hook in the opposite direction from the spiral **(i)**. Finish by making a tiny loop at the end of the hook and squeezing it closed with chainnose pliers **(j)**.

5 Place each spiral component and the hook on a bench block, and use a chasing hammer to flatten and work-harden them **(k)**.

6 Place the bottom half of a rivet on the bench block. Place a spiral component over the rivet half so that the rivet protrudes through the center of the spiral. Then place a bead cap or spacer on the rivet, and set the top half of the rivet in place. Carefully hammer with a riveting hammer until the rivet holds firmly **(l)**. Repeat this step with the remaining spiral components and hook.

7 Open and close pairs of 3 mm jump rings (Basics, p. 110) to connect the spiral components and hook. At the end of the bracelet opposite the hook, use two pairs of 3 mm jump rings to attach a 6 mm jump ring, which will be the eye for the hook.

note

Follow the instructions for the earrings to make a drop pendant, but instead of attaching an ear wire in step 6, connect the pendant to the loop of a bail. You can scale your pendant up or down as desired by using more or less wire and making a larger or smaller spiral — try experimenting!

Crazy Eights Celtic Ring

Update the timeless infinity symbol
in a contemporary ring.

by Dawn Horner

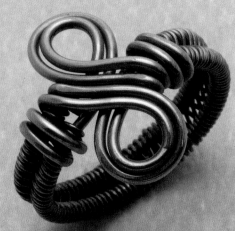

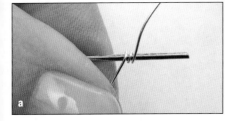

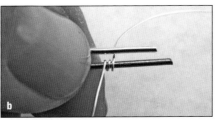

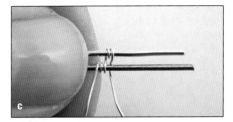

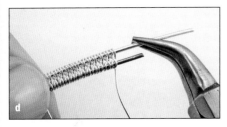

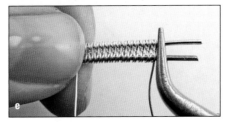

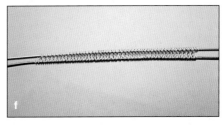

materials

Ring with ¾ x ½-in. (19 x 38 mm) focal

- Copper, sterling, or colored/plated wire, round, dead soft:
  - 16 in. (40.6 cm) 18-gauge (1.0 mm)
  - 3½–4 ft. (1.1–1.2 m) 26-gauge (0.4 mm)

tools & supplies

- Wirework toolbox, p. 105
- Ring mandrel

Woven ring band

1 Flush-cut two 8-in. (20.3 cm) pieces of 18-gauge (base) wire. Cut 3½–4 ft. (1.1–1.2 m) of 26-gauge (wrapping) wire.

TIP

For ring sizes 8 and larger, use 4 ft. (1.2 m) of 26-gauge wire.

2 Hold one base wire in your non-dominant hand. With the same hand, use your thumb and forefinger to hold the wrapping wire perpendicular to the base and 1 in. (25.5 mm) from the end. With your dominant hand, make two wraps around the base wire, wrapping away from you **(a)**.

3 Hold the second base wire above and parallel to the first, on top of the wrapping wire. Leave a 3 mm gap between the two base wires **(b)**. Make two wraps around the second base wire, wrapping toward you. Bring the wrapping wire under the first base wire **(c)**.

4 Continue making two wraps around each base wire, forming a figure-8 weave. Keep only about 1 in. (25.5 mm) of each base wire exposed while weaving. Use pliers to pull out more of the base wires when less than 1 in. (25.5 mm) is exposed **(d)**. Occasionally use your fingers and pliers to gently compress the weave from each end **(e)**.

TIP

To determine the length of the woven section for the ring band, measure the circumference of a ring mandrel at your ring size, and subtract ⅛ in. (3 mm). Example: For ring size 7, the circumference of the mandrel is 2⅛ in. (54 mm), so make a 2-in. (51 mm) woven section.

5 When the woven section is the desired length, center the weave on the base wires. There will be about 3 in. (76 mm) of exposed base wires on each end. Trim and tuck each end of the wrapping wire (Basics, p. 109) **(f)**.

Crazy Eights focal

6 Bend the band around a ring mandrel so that the base wires meet and are centered at one size larger than the desired ring size. (The band size will decrease as you make the focal.) Hold the mandrel and the band so that the ends of the base wires are facing you. If you're right-handed, the top pair of base wires should come from the right **(g)**. If you're left-handed, the top pair of base wires should come from the left.

7 Hold the band on the mandrel with your nondominant hand, and use your thumb to firmly hold the base wires where they meet. With your dominant hand, gently curve the top pair of base wires clockwise, allowing the curve to tighten into what would appear to be one end of an oval **(h)**.

8 Remove the ring from the mandrel, and pull the base wires downward, using bentnose pliers if needed **(i)**. This creates an upside-down teardrop shape. Center the teardrop so that the base wires extend across the lower pair of base wires at a 7 o'clock position **(j)**.

TIPS

- You can use finger tape to protect your fingertips when working with wire.
- Apply Tool Magic to the tips of your pliers to keep them from marring the wire.

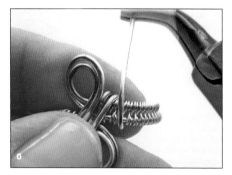

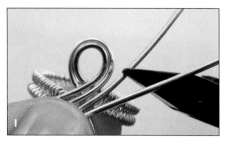

TIP

The teardrop will be more uniform if you shape it to the left of your thumb and then gently center it once you've formed it. If the woven section has shifted on the base wires during this procedure, reposition it.

9 Turn the ring upside down, and place it back on the mandrel at about ¾ of a size larger than the desired ring size. Repeat steps 7 and 8, and then adjust the pair of teardrops as desired **(k)**.

Compress or stretch the woven section of the band so it's a half-size larger than the desired ring size (this will allow space for finishing). Remove the ring from the mandrel.

10 Flush-cut one of the inner base wires, leaving a ⅛–¼-in. (3–6.5 mm) tail extending past the band **(l)**. Use round-nose pliers to form a hook at the tip of the tail, and tuck it inside the woven section of the band **(m)**. Repeat to cut and secure the other inner base wire.

11 Place the ring on the mandrel. Use a chasing hammer to gently tap the center of the focal to set the wires in place **(n)**.

12 Wrap each of the outer base wires twice around the band, ending with the wire pointing away from you **(o)**. Repeat step 10 to cut and secure each outer base wire **(p)**.

13 Use roundnose pliers to gently curve the top and bottom of the focal so that it lies flush against your finger when worn **(q)**.

BASICS

ABOUT WIRE

Buying wire is fairly easy, but it's best to know a little about your choices before you buy. Try to buy the most appropriate material for your project. You'll find that some wires work better than others for different purposes. Understanding the materials, shapes, and gauges of wire can make wireworking that much more successful.

Wire is available in a wide range of materials. Gold and silver are the most traditional choices, but wire also is available in brass, copper, and niobium, among other options. When you are first starting out, you may want to try copper or inexpensive craft wire to learn techniques such as coiling or making hooks. These wires are easy to manipulate and much less expensive than silver or gold.

Silver

There are four common options for silver wire: fine silver, sterling silver, Argentium silver, and German silver. Of these, fine silver is the purest, composed almost entirely of silver. However, fine silver is a fairly soft material, so it is not ideal for certain jewelry elements, such as clasps, closures, or hooks, which take a lot of

stress. If certain elements don't require a lot of strength, such as a head pin for hanging a single bead, use fine silver. It will stay white and lustrous without much polishing since it oxidizes at a slow rate. It also doesn't have to be pickled after heating if used without flux.

Sterling silver and Argentium silver are perfect for most jewelry-making applications, since they have been alloyed with other metals for additional strength. Sterling silver has long been the material of choice for jewelry makers, since it is strong and malleable. Sterling silver is 92.5% fine silver with 7.5% copper and other metals—thus the .925 stamp on sterling. The drawback to sterling is this small copper content makes it oxidize at a faster rate than fine silver, so it tends to tarnish quickly. Argentium silver is an alloy that substitutes a higher content of germanium to avoid the tarnishing problem while retaining the strength of the metal. Argentium has the best qualities of sterling without its oxidation rate, but Argentium is a bit stiffer than sterling to work with.

German silver wire is frequently found in beading stores and craft shops. This wire is formed by layering sterling silver over a copper core. The copper makes the wire very malleable and easy to use, but if you have exposed wire ends (as on wrapped loops), or if you need to hammer your wire, the copper core of the wire will show. For that reason, many jewelry makers avoid German silver wire.

Gold

Gold wire is available in different karat weights, tempers (see p. 104), and even colors. 24k gold is pure gold, but very soft to work with, while 14k gold is a 7/12-gold alloy. For those of you who love the warm,

silken appearance of gold but want to keep the costs of your jewelry-making endeavors affordable, gold-filled wire is an economical choice. It's a fraction of the cost of 14k-gold wire. Contrary to its name, gold-filled wire is actually gold overlay. A thin layer of 24k gold is heat- and pressure-bonded to a brass core. The layer of pure gold makes the wire tarnish-resistant, and it should be cared for just like the expensive version. Gold-filled wire should be buffed with a soft, clean cloth (such as flannel) and stored in a dry place. Placing tissue paper around your gold-filled wire will minimize exposure to humidity and prevent scratching while it's being stored.

Gold-plated wire exists, but only a microscopic film of karat gold is applied to the outside of the wire, rather than an actual layer.

Temper

The temper of wire is its hardness, or malleability. Silver and gold wires can be purchased at different levels of hardness, such as dead-soft, half-hard, or full-hard. When working with metal, you want it to be pliable enough to manipulate, yet strong enough to hold its shape. Working with wire strengthens it; this is called work-hardening. Additional strength comes with hammering after you've formed your shape. The trick is to use wire that is soft enough to work with but becomes hard enough to hold the final shape.

You likely will want to work with half-hard wire the majority of the time. When connecting elements with double-wrapped loops, the act of wrapping the loops is enough manipulation to fully work-harden the wire so it is at its maximum strength. If you used full-hard

Wire gauge conversion chart		
Gauge size	Diameter (in.)	Diameter (mm)
10	0.102	2.6
12	0.081	2.1
14	0.064	1.6
16	0.051	1.3
18	0.040	1.0
20	0.032	0.8
22	0.025	0.6
24	0.020	0.5
26	0.016	0.4
28	0.013	0.32
30	0.010	0.26

wire, it could be too difficult to manipulate. If you use dead-soft wire, it could only become half-hard after wrapping, so it would not maintain its shape as well. Most projects in this book will specify which temper works best for each project.

Gauge

Wire gauge is the measure of a wire's thickness or diameter. The higher the gauge number, the thinner the wire. Thicker wire is more difficult to work with, while thinner wire has less strength.

Thick wire, such as 12- and 14-gauge wire, is most appropriate for projects where strength is a necessary element of the design, such as bangle bracelets.

For projects and components that need to be strong, but not quite as sturdy or bulky —such as clasps—16- and 18-gauge wire is more appropriate. 20- and 22-gauge wire is commonly used for most jewelry-making elements, and is perfect for loops and findings. Finer wires are used with small-holed beads, or for decorative elements.

An American-standard wire gauge (see top left picture)displays gauges on one side and the corresponding-diameter decimal measurements on the other. A gauge is measured by the width of each slot on the perimeter of the tool, not by the size of the hole.

Shape

Wire also comes in a variety of shapes, ranging from the traditional round profile to half-round, flat or square, triangular, and twisted. (You can make your own twisted wire by twisting two pieces together.)

TOOLS

If you love tools, there's no limit to what you can buy. The jewelry-making world keeps finding more and better ways to create beautiful pieces. The essentials that you absolutely have to have are pliers and cutters. We've included some of the more fundamental tools here in a handy toolbox.

Wirework toolbox
- Bench block or anvil
- Cup bur or wire rounder
- Cutters: side, end, or flush
- Hammers: chasing, ball peen, cross peen
- Mallet: rawhide or plastic
- Mandrels or dowels
- Needle files
- Pliers: chainnose, flatnose, roundnose, parallel, nylon jaw
- Polishing cloth
- Sandpaper: various grits
- Tumbler, steel shot, burnishing compound

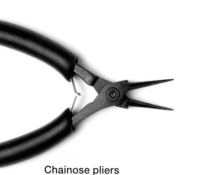

Chainose pliers

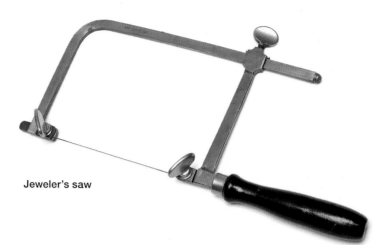

Jeweler's saw

Flatnose pliers

Bentnose pliers

Nylon-jaw pliers

Roundnose pliers

Pliers

Pliers are necessary for most wire working tasks, including gripping and bending wire, and creating loops. There are also many specialty pliers, such as stone-setters, ring openers, and combinations that might be perfect for your needs. When purchasing pliers, inspect the jaws to see that they are smooth and even, look for a solid joint with a little give or wiggle, and try out the handle. Here are some of the basic types of pliers.

Chainnose pliers have flat inner jaws, great for gripping wire to shape it, or working in conjunction with another type of pliers, to make loops or to open and close jump rings.

Flatnose pliers are similar to chainnose pliers and can be used in the same manner, but have flat outer jaws, making it easier to make sharper bends in the wire.

Bentnose or bent chainnose pliers are also close to chainnose pliers, but have a slight bend near the tips. Many jewelry makers prefer these pliers because they find them easier to use than the straight chainnose variety.

Nylon-jaw pliers are another relative of chainnose pliers. These pliers feature replaceable nylon lining on the jaws, which protects wire from marks left by tools and is useful for straightening wire. You can achieve similar results by covering your pliers with tape or Tool Magic,

but eventually wear and tear will affect the protection those aids offer. These are particularly useful with wires that have a thin coating of color that could easily scratch off, such as niobium.

Roundnose pliers are critical for making loops and bends. These pliers have conical jaws, perfect for shaping wire.

Saws

Jeweler's saws have two components: an adjustable U-shaped frame with a handle and a blade. You can use a variety of different blade sizes or thicknesses in the saw; use stronger blades for thicker metal. Saws are great for cutting shapes from metal and sawing through coils to make jump rings.

Cutters

Depending on the type of work you do, you'll need different cutters for your jewelry making. If you file all your ends, a stronger cutter with a less refined finish is appropriate. If you use a lot of jump rings, a saw is essential.

Side cutters are the most common type of cutters. As the name implies, these cutters have blades that are parallel to their handles. Some side cutters have blades that are tilted slightly upward. These are useful because they can cut wire from many angles. All the cutters included here are usually found as side cutters. End cutters, which have blades set perpendicular to the handles, are not usually used for wirework.

| Bevel cutters | Semi-flush cutters | Flush cutters | Super-flush cutters |

Bevel cutters are economical, can cut very thick gauges of wire, and last longer than many other types of cutters. However, bevel cutters leave both ends of your wire pinched at a slant. (Hence the word "bevel," which means "an incline or slant.") Also, you must squeeze bevel cutters harder than some other types of side cutters. If you want the ends of your wires to be flat, you will have to file them.

Semi-flush cutters leave less of a slant or bur on wire ends than bevel cutters. One side of the cut will be almost flush, while the other side will be beveled. These cutters are good for beginners to use.

Flush cutters leave even less of a bevel, and super-flush (aka ultra-flush) cutters are even better than flush cutters. They produce a flatter cut and require even less energy to use. However, in exchange for their tremendous cutting ability, super-flush cutters lose strength, so you can use them only for wire finer than 18-gauge.

Double-flush cutters leave virtually no bur on either side of the wire, saving you time if you want your wire ends to be perfectly flat. Double-flush cutters work well for making jump rings from wire coils. As you might expect, double-flush cutters work only on thinner gauges of wire, 18-gauge and finer.

Hammers and mallets

While one hammer might be sufficient for beginners, there's a wide variety of jewelry-making hammers out there, and some will make certain tasks much easier.

Ball-peen and cross-peen hammers are the most common jewelry-making hammers. Ball-peen hammers have flat heads on one end, and domed round heads on the other. Cross-peen hammers have a rectangular head instead of the round head. These hammers are great for shaping and texturing metal.

A chasing hammer is struck against tools, like stamps and punches, to make indentations and marks on the metal. It is a modified version of the ball-peen hammer.

A riveting hammer can also be used with tools, or to add texture to a piece of metal, but its real purpose is to shape and flatten the rivets used in cold connections. The angled head pushes the metal out with each blow, flaring the rivet heads.

A planishing hammer smooths and flattens the surface of metal. Although other hammers can be used for this purpose, planishing hammers have two flat, round, smooth heads. Keep your planishing heads smooth by never using them with your steel tools. The hard steel will mar the shiny surfaces.

Nylon and rawhide mallets are used to pound and form metal without marking it. The head materials cushion the metal while it's being struck. Some rawhide mallets need to be conditioned before they are used, so they don't leave marks.

Rawhide mallet

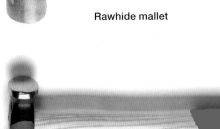

Planishing hammer

Riveting hammer

Chasing hammer

Ball-peen hammer

Bench block

Dapping block

Torch

Files

Bench blocks and anvils

A bench block, or steel block, provides a hard, smooth surface on which to hammer or planish your pieces. An anvil is similarly hard, but has different surfaces, such as a tapered horn, to help forge wire into different shapes.

Dapping block

A dapping block, or doming block, is a steel block with a series of concave circles set into its surface. You can use a mallet in conjunction with dapping punches to pound metal pieces into the indentations, giving them a rounded form.

Dowels and mandrels

Dowels are circular rods, frequently made of wood, that jewelry makers use for shaping wire into coils and rings. Mandrels are made of steel, plastic, or wood, and have a smooth or stepped taper, so that rings and coils can be easily measured and removed. Jewelry makers are frequently creative with their dowels and mandrels and often use other tools, like punches or knitting needles, as dowels and mandrels.

Drills and punches

Drills and punches are used together to make holes in metal surfaces. First, a center punch (a steel rod with a pointed end) is used to make a dimple in the metal where the hole will be drilled. This dimple keeps the drill bit in place, so it doesn't travel over the surface of the metal and mar it. Then the drill is used to create the hole itself.

Torches

Torches are necessary for annealing and soldering wire components. They differ greatly in price range, temperature, and fuel. A wealth of material on torches is available, and those interested in using one should seek advice from trusted, knowledgeable sources.

Files

Metal files are used to refine and shape the edges of metal and wire surfaces. In most cases, they are essential for professional-looking jewelry.

BASIC TECHNIQUES

Pickling

Pickle is an acidic solution used for removing oxides and flux from metal. Mix it according to the manufacturer's instructions, and warm it in a Crock-Pot (which you mustn't use for food again!) or in a container on a hot plate. Using copper, wooden, or plastic tongs (not steel), submerge and remove your piece as needed to clean your metal.

Coiling

Wire can be wrapped around a mandrel, dowel, or core wire to make a coil. Tools like the Coiling Gizmo make the job fast and easy, but for small jobs, or when you're coiling onto a wire already in your project, you can do it by hand.

To make a coil, hold the coiling wire perpendicular to the mandrel or core wire. Wrap the wire around the core until the coil is the desired length. Keep the wraps close to each other to prevent gaps in the coil.

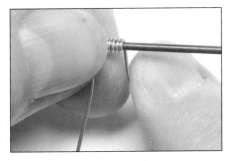

Forming spirals

1 Grasp the end of a wire with the tips of roundnose pliers, and rotate the pliers to form a small loop.

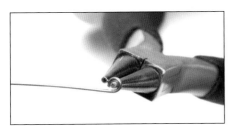

2 Grasp across the loop with chainnose or flatnose pliers, and use your fingers to guide the wire tail around the loop. Continue rotating until the spiral is the desired size.

3 Leaving a bit of space between the rotations will give you an open spiral (left); leaving no space will give you a tight spiral (right).

Trimming and tucking wire

When you finish wrapping one wire around another, use flush cutters to trim the wrapping wire close to your work. Use chainnose pliers to press down or "tuck" the very end of the wrapped wire so it doesn't stick out. Whenever possible, trim and tuck wire on the back of your work to hide the end and prevent snags.

Twisting square wire

Twisting square wire gives it a pretty, ornate look. You'll get the most consistent results if you twist short lengths of wire (10 in./25.4 cm or less) at a time.

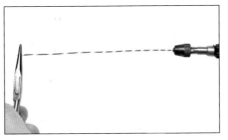

To twist wire, insert one end into the chuck of a pin vise or electric drill. Holding the other end of the wire firmly with flat-nose pliers, rotate the pin vise or start the electric drill at a slow speed. Continue until the twist is consistent along the length of the wire.

Work-hardening wire

For added strength, it is often beneficial to work-harden wire. There are a few ways to do this. One option is to form the wire into the desired shape and then hammer it. If you also want to flatten the wire somewhat, use a chasing hammer or a ball-peen hammer. If you want to work-harden the wire without flattening it, use a plastic or rawhide mallet.

Another option is to run the wire through a pair of nylon-jaw pliers. This also straightens the wire, so you would do this before shaping or bending it.

Loops and wraps
Plain loop

1 If making a plain loop above a bead, trim the wire ³⁄₈ in. (9.5 mm) above the bead. Using chain-nose pliers, make a right-angle bend close to the bead. If working with a naked piece of wire, make a bend ¼ in. (6.5 mm) from the end.

2 Grasp the tip of the wire with roundnose pliers, and roll the wire to form a half-circle.

3 Reposition the pliers in the loop, and continue rolling, forming a centered circle above the bead.

4 This is the finished loop.

Wrapped loop

1 If making a wrapped loop above a bead, make sure there is at least 1¼ in. (32 mm) of wire above the bead. With the tip of your chainnose pliers, grasp the wire directly above the bead. Bend the wire above the pliers into a right angle. If working with a naked piece of wire, make a bend 1¼ in. (32 mm) from the end.

2 Position the jaws of your roundnose pliers in the bend. Bring the wire over the top jaw of the pliers.

3 Reposition the pliers' lower jaw snugly in the curved wire. Wrap the wire down and around the bottom of the pliers. This is the first half of a wrapped loop.

4 Grasp the loop with chainnose pliers.

5 Wrap the wire tail around the stem, covering the stem between the loop and the top of the bead. Trim and tuck the excess wire (see "Trimming and tucking wire," p. 109).

Finishing

Tumble-polishing

Place steel shot into the tumbler's barrel. Although you can use any shape of steel shot, a combination of shapes works best; the various shapes polish crevices and contours differently, ensuring an even polish.

Pour in enough water to cover the shot, and add a bit of burnishing compound or dish soap. Place your jewelry in the tumbler, and seal the barrel. Turn on the tumbler, and let it run for two hours or more. Pour the contents of the tumbler into a sieve over a sink, and rinse. Remove your jewelry, and dry it. Dry the shot before storing it

Patinating (darkening metal) with liver of sulfur

Polish your piece before patinating. (If you tumble-polish your piece after patinating, reserve the used shot for future patinated pieces; the liver of sulfur residue will contaminate non-patinated pieces.) Oil and dirt on the piece can affect the patina, so clean the metal with degreasing soap first.

Prepare a liver of sulfur solution according to the manufacturer's instructions. Dip the metal in the solution for a few seconds, and then rinse the metal in cool water to stop the chemical reaction. For a darker patina, continue to dip and rinse the metal. Use a brass brush with soapy water to remove or modify the patina. For different colors of patina, experiment with different temperatures and amounts of water to make the solution.

Making and using jump rings

Coiling jump rings by hand

Select a wooden dowel or mandrel with a diameter that matches the inside diameter of the jump rings you want. Drill a hole through one end of the dowel. Insert the end of the wire into the hole. Coil the wire around the dowel (see "Coiling," p. 109).

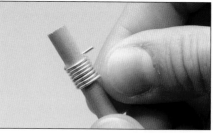

Cut the wire that anchors the coil. If you will be using wire cutters to cut the coil into jump rings, remove the coil from the dowel. If you will be using a jeweler's saw, slide the coil to the opposite end of the dowel (see "Cutting jump rings using a jeweler's saw," right).

Cutting jump rings using wire cutters

1 Holding the flush-cut edge of your cutters at a right angle to the coil, trim the straight wire tail from each end of the coil.
2 Slightly separate the first ring from the coil. Holding the flush-cut edge of your cutters at a right angle to the coil, cut where the wire completes the first ring. If you use diagonal wire cutters, one end of

your ring will be flush and the other end will be pointed. To flush-cut the pointed end, flip your cutters over to the flush-cut side, and cut again so that both cuts are flush. (Because of this extra cut, there will be some wire waste, so make a few extra coils to make up for it.) Continue cutting rings from the coil.

Cutting jump rings using a jeweler's saw

Secure the dowel against the V notch in your bench pin, and use a jeweler's saw with a 2/0 blade to cut a shallow, vertical slot at the end of the dowel to guide your blade as you cut the coil. Hold the coil and dowel with your non-dominant hand. Saw through the top of the coil, feeding it toward the slot in the dowel. Be careful not to cut the jump rings in half.

Opening and closing a jump ring or loop

1 Hold the jump ring with two pairs of pliers, such as chainnose, flatnose, and/or bentnose. To open the jump ring, bring one pair of pliers toward you, and push the other pair away from you. Do not pull the jump ring open sideways.

2 To close the jump ring, reverse the direction of the pliers to bring the ends of the jump ring back together. Because jump rings (especially those used in chain mail) tend to spring back, you may find it helpful to bring the tips of the ring a bit past the closed position and then bring them back together. Apply the same technique for opening all plain loops, such as earring wires.

CONTRIBUTORS

Janice Berkebile is a wire/metal artist who teaches at Fusion Beads in her hometown of Seattle, Wash., and in bead stores across the country. Janice has written a book, *Making Wire & Bead Jewelry*, and launched a website, Wired Arts (www.wiredarts.net), with fellow Seattle artist Tracy Stanley.

Zoraida Bros is a self-taught artist and is inspired by nature and artistic creations of ancient cultures. Email her at zbmarket@ gmail.com, or visit www.zoraida jewelry.com and www.zoraida. artfire.com.

Lilian Chen is an internationally known wire artist, and the founder of the "sketch style" wireworking method. She teaches frequently. Email her at rhombusga@gmail. com, or see more of her work at www.pinterest.com/goldgatsby desig/wire-sculpture-3d-sketch-style-wire-sculpture.

Lisa Claxton began making beaded jewelry in high school, and she learned new skills and techniques when she worked at a bead store after college. Lisa is a full-time studio artist and jewelry instructor. To see more of her work, visit www.lisaclaxton.com.

Monica Han is an award-winning mixed-media jewelry designer and teacher in Potomac, Md. Contact her via e-mail at monicaleehan@ yahoo.com.

Dawn Horner of Wasilla, Alaska, strives to preserve and incorporate ancient metal and wire techniques in her work. She enjoys teaching people not only how to make jewelry, but also the history behind these techniques. Email Dawn at northernadornments@gmail.com, or to see more of her work, visit www.northernadornments.com.

Lisa Niven Kelly is an award-winning artist who finds joy in all things beads. Lisa is a regular contributor to many jewelry-making magazines and is the author of the book *Stamped Metal Jewelry*. She has been teaching beadwork and wirework for more than 15 years. These days you will find Lisa sticking close to home with her two young daughters and managing her business, Beaducation.com.

Colette Kimon has been making jewelry for about eight years and always enjoys creating in her spare time—that is, when she's not busy with her children! Contact Colette at www.colettecollection.com.

Tracey Knaus is a self-taught wire artist based in Calgary, Alberta, Canada. She was accepted into the Alberta College of Art & Design for Jewelry Design, but chose a career in aviation instead. Now a stay-at-home mom, she is pursuing her dream and developing her artistic skills and business. Find her on Facebook and Artfire by searching "Wares Tracey."

Lisa Liddy has been making jewelry for several years. She particularly enjoys designing jewelry that highlights art-glass beads. Lisa sells her jewelry and supplies through her Etsy site, www.joolzbylisa.etsy.com. You can e-mail her at joolzbylisa@cox.net.

Melody MacDuffee has been making bead and wire jewelry for more than 20 years. Many of her pieces are inspired by her work as the Executive Director of Soul of Somanya, a nonprofit organization that helps young Krobo artists in Ghana to create and market their products. Melody has written several books, including *Lacy Wire Jewelry* and *Decorative Wire Findings*, published by Kalmbach Publishing Co. To contact Melody, visit www.soulofsomanya.net.

Gretchen McHale is a jewelry designer and event planner from Philadelphia. She's been making jewelry for more than 28 years and sells it through her website, www.studio320jewelry.com. You can contact her at gretchen@ studio320jewelry.com.

Irina Miech has been involved in jewelry making for more than 20 years. She has authored numerous jewelry design books, including *Beautiful Wire Jewelry for Beaders*, volumes 1 and 2. She owns the retail bead store Eclectica in Brookfield, Wis., and offers classes in wirework and metal clay. Contact her at info@eclectica beads.com.

Erin Paton has been making jewelry for about 10 years. She enjoys wirework because of the endless possibilities for creating a piece without solder. Erin sells her work at www.earringsbyerin. etsy.com. Contact her at earrings byerin@gmail.com.

Debra Saucier has been making jewelry for more than 10 years. She loves making sculptural wire pieces because she enjoys the structure and lines created by square wire. When she's not making jewelry, Debra spends time with her husband and three kids. To see more of Debra's work, visit www.debrasaucier.com.

Brenda Schweder Brenda Schweder is an artist, author, teacher, creativity columnist, and now, inventor of Now That's a Jig!, the wire bending system that Sits Tight and Stays Put! She's written three books. Her designs and fashion jewelry forecasts have been published over 100 times in books and magazines. Visit her websites at www.BrendaSchweder.com and www.Now-That's-a-Jig.com and catch her on Etsy, Facebook, YouTube, and Pinterest.

Eva Sherman has discovered an affinity for working with wire and metals, and prefers to design in an unstructured style. Eva is the co-author of *Organic Wire and Metal Jewelry*, published by Kalmbach Publishing Co. Contact Eva at grandriverbeads@sbcglobal.net, or visit www.grandriverbeads.com.

Melissa Grakowsky Shippee fell in love with beading in 2007. While illustrating the book *Bewitching Bead & Wire Jewelry*, she received a crash course in wire-wrapping techniques and has begun making wire creations of her own. Melissa teaches beaded jewelry workshops all over the world and sells patterns through her website, www.mgs designs.net.

Donna Spadafore's journey in wire jewelry began with a paper clip, a pair of pliers, and a few minutes of boredom. See Donna's jewelry at www.etsy.com/shop/ GailaviraJewelry or purchase tutorials for other designs at www. etsy.com/shop/GailaviraTutorials.

Barb Switzer has been making jewelry for 15 years and started working with wire after a good friend gave her tools and wire as a birthday gift. She enjoys weaving and shaping wire and turning a simple line into a three-dimensional structure. Contact Barb at beadswitzer@yahoo.com.

Hana Terpo grew up in the Czech Republic, and has spent her whole life making creative use of her mind and hands. In 2004, she began making jewelry that blends a natural aesthetic with long-term wear. Her favorite materials are gold, copper, silver, wood, stone, pearl and leather. Although wirework is her favorite technique, she also dabbles in metalwork. Hana makes jewelry to relax after a hectic job with Apple. See more of her work at www.fidana.etsy.com or contact her at fidana@me.com.

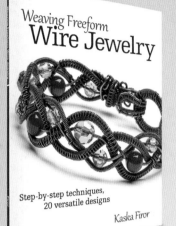

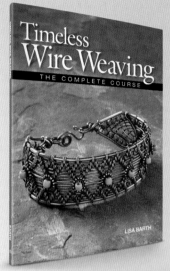